BIKE ACROSS AMERICA
1965
FINDING MY FATHER

BIKE ACROSS
AMERICA
1965
FINDING MY FATHER

NORM HANSEN

The author has tried to recreate events, locations, and conversations from his memories of them. In order to maintain the historical accuracy of this work, the author has chosen to keep in language that may be offensive/sensitive to some readers.

ISBN: 978-0-578-95164-5 – Hardcover

Library of Congress Control Number: 2021914105   0 8 0 6 2 1

♾ This paper meets the requirements of ANSI/NISO Z39.48-1992 (Permanence of Paper)

Cover Designer by Ariel Thieken
Custom Map by Shane Coursen

BIKE ACROSS AMERICA, 1965

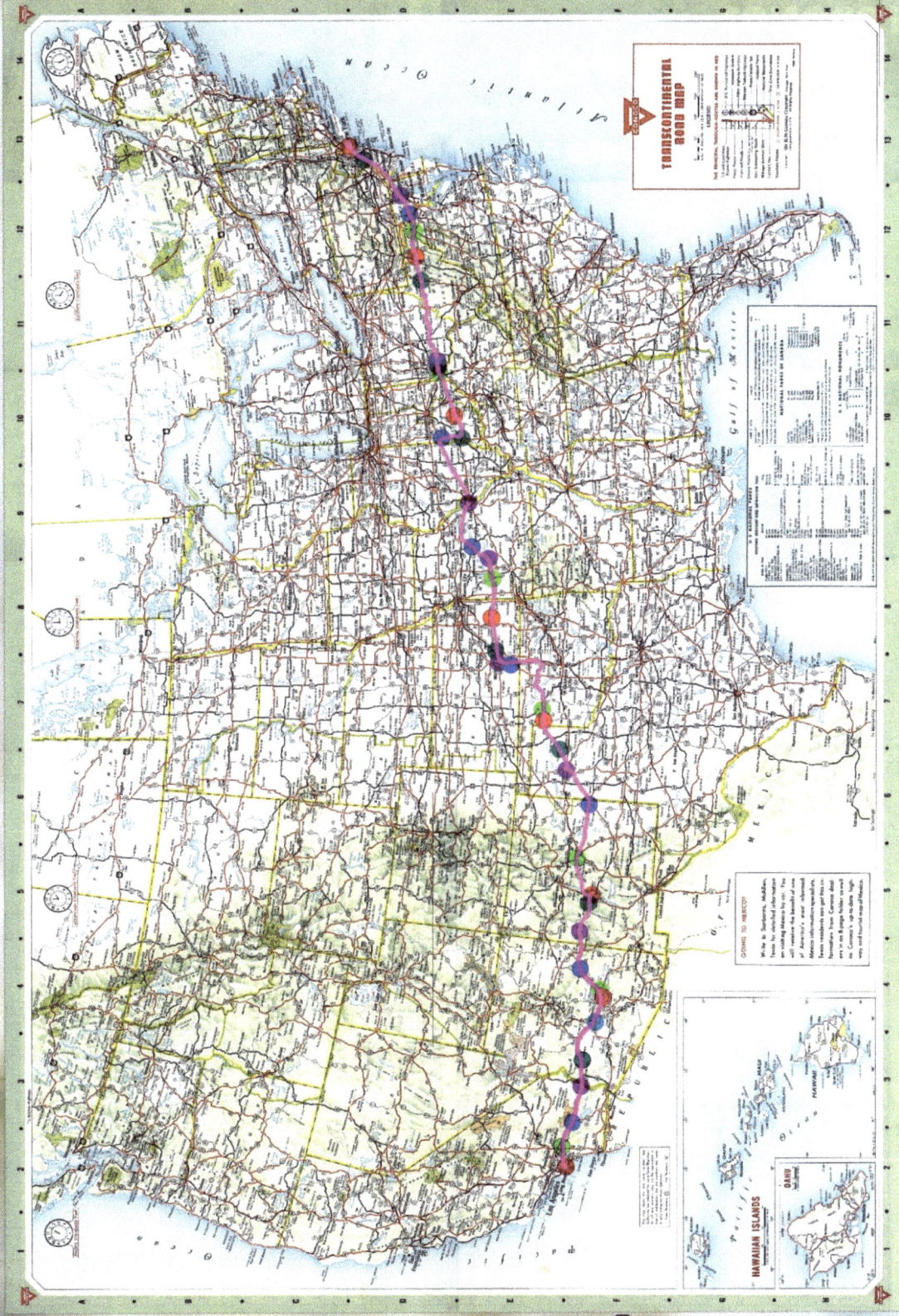

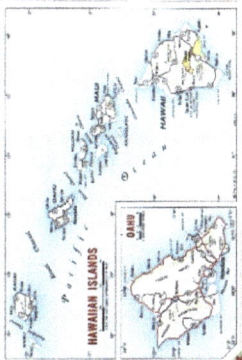

DAY 11
MOUNTAINAIR, NM / SOCORRO, NM

DAY 12
ENCINO, NM

DAY 13
CLOVIS, NM

DAY 14
AMARILLO, TX

DAY 15
AMARILLO REST DAY

DAY 16
PAMPA, TX

DAY 17
ARNETT, OK

DAY 18
FAIRVIEW, OK

DAY 19
CALDWELL, KS

DAY 20
WICHITA, KS

DAY 21
EL DORADO, KS

DAY 22
IOLA, KS

DAY 23
COLLINS, MO

DAY 24
CAMDENTON, MO

DAY 25
JEFFERSON CITY, MO

DAY 9
QUEMADO, AZ

DAY 10
MAGDALENA, NM

DAY 7
GLOBE, AZ

DAY 8
SHOW LOW, AZ

DAY 26
[SALVATION ARMY]
JEFFERSON, MO

DAY 27
UNION, MO/ST. LOUIS, MO

DAY 28
W. CARLYLE, IL

DAY 29
VINCENNES, IN

DAY 5
PHOENIX, AZ

DAY 6
REST & REPAIR

DAY 30
BEDFORD, IN

DAY 31
CINCINNATI, OH

DAY 3
BLYTH, CA

DAY 4
SALOME, AZ

DAY 32
CAMPGROUND IN OH

DAY 33
CLARKSBURG, WV

DAY 1
DEPART
NEWPORT BEACH, CA

ARRIVE
ELSINORE, CA

DAY 2
INDIO, CA

DAY 42: WORLD'S FAIR
FLUSHING MEADOWS PARK
QUEENS, NY

DAY 40-41
ST. GEORGE HOTEL
NEW YORK, NY

DAY 39
NORRISTOWN, PA

DAY 38
GETTYSBURG BATTLEFIELD
[IN SLEEPING BAGS]

DAY 37
MARTINSBURG, PA / GETTYSBURG, PA

DAY 36
GETTYSBURG, PA

DAY 35
POTOMAC RIVER / WINCHESTER, VA

DAY 34
WINCHESTER, VA

Departure from Newport Beach
May 1, 1965

PROLOGUE

To New York World's Fair/In Search of My Father

The summer of 1965 was well before the start of the TET Offensive in 1968. We were going to win the war now, so they told us! Of course, I was draft status 1A and yes, I was going to be drafted.

I spent the previous two years training for the 1964 Olympic Games, Cycling Road Racing Event on a 1963 Schwinn Paramount and a Bianchi racing bike and did not make the cut. At the time, there were two types of bikes: the Paramount, which Schwinn supplied for the road-racing team, and paper-route bicycles, which have one speed and weigh about fifty pounds with coaster brakes. This bike trip took place prior to the bike craze. It was not yet cool to be peddling a bike, and this was ten years before the start of the interstate highway systems. Roads were bad and had no shoulders. Bike lanes were not even an idea.

I was lost. Vietnam was in my future, my girlfriend dumped me, I had just graduated from junior college with no money and no job. How was I going to pay for my acceptance to California State, Long Beach?

I tried smoking pot with a friend, but that didn't work since I was allergic to the smoke. So now what?

I never mentioned to Butch why I was doing this trip. I wanted to find my father!

Butch was an adopted child and I thought it might hurt his feelings if I told him. I was ashamed that my real father had never reached out to me. I was hoping my father would see the news articles and respond.

A relative of mine in New York called and said he had a friend with a concession stand at the 1964–65 New York World's Fair. His friend would get us tickets to the fair, a place to stay, and tickets home if we would ride our bikes out there for publicity before the summer started. May 1 would be the starting date. AAA planned the route, and the news media was informed. So I was committed.

My thought was, I was going to Vietnam where I could get killed so I figured I might as well have some fun before that could happen. Getting run over by a Buick would probably be less painful!

We prepared the bikes as duplicates except for the tires. Spare spokes, chain links, cables, and tools for truing wheels. Spare tires with repair patch kits. We replaced the rear freewheel cluster with a 14–28 tooth. It was called a touring cluster. Both bikes were the same size and weight. The crank length size was slightly different and almost ruined the trip.

I wanted to keep a daily journal because we didn't know what we would encounter on this epic, one-of-a-kind journey. So, I bought a little, red, daily-reminder journal.

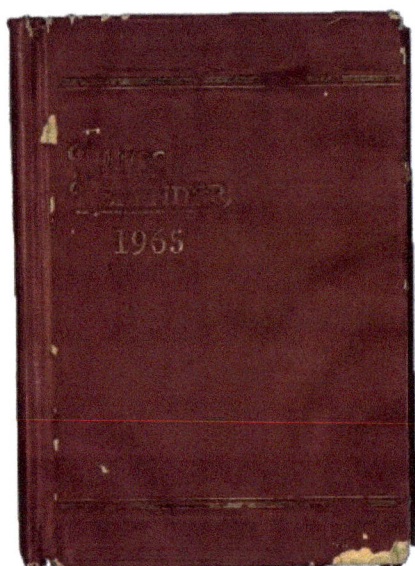

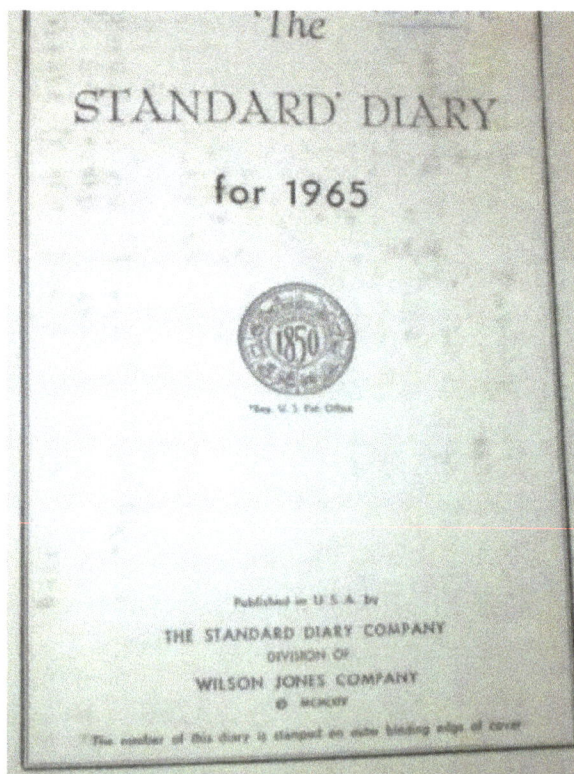

1963 SCHWINN PARAMOUNT

Weight: *22.5 lbs*
Price: *$175.00 (new)*

5 Speed Regina Rear Cluster

USA Olympic Emblem & Schwinn Paramount Seal

Chain Ring & Rat Traps/Pedals

Brooks Saddle

Glued on Sew-Up Tires (left) Sew-Up Tire Repair Kit (right)

There's Nothing Finer

Schwinn Paramount Road Racer

Schwinn's finest road racing
sports bike . . . with
10-speed derailleur, lightweight
steel alloy frame, racing wheels
with aluminum alloy rims,
center pull caliper brakes,
racing handlebars, racing
saddle, rattrap pedals.
Choice of 21, 22, 23 or
24 inch frame sizes.

No.	Size	Description	Shpg. Wt. Lbs.
P12	27 inch	10-Speed Paramount Road Racer	25

COLORS: Any Schwinn color.
OPTIONAL AT EXTRA COST
1. White Plastic Mudguards
2. Campagnolo Seat Post
3. Campagnolo Gran-Sport Pedals
4. Campagnolo Record Alloy Crank Set
5. Chrome Plate Finish—(a) Partial: Fork Crown and sides, rear forks, stays and head lugs; or (b) full chrome.
6. Custom-built made-to-measure frame (Write for special order form)

OTHER PARAMOUNT MODELS (Not Illustrated)

No.	Size	Description	Shpg. Wt. Lbs.
P13	27 inch	Men's Paramount Tourist	28
P61	27 inch	Ladies' Paramount Tourist	28
P15	27 inch	Men's Paramount Track Bike	22

Touring models in choice of 10-speed, 3-speed, free-wheel or coaster brake . . . equipped with plastic fenders, mattress saddle, and touring handlebars. Track bikes are custom-built. Write for complete information.

SPECIFICATIONS

Frame:	Reynolds 531 butted tubing, Nervex lugs
Wheels:	Weinmann aluminum alloy rims, Campagnolo Record quick release hubs
Tires:	Dunlop 27" x 1¼" road racing, or tubular sew-up . . . Please specify
Handlebar:	Aluminum alloy drop handlebars, steel stem
Brakes:	Weinmann center-pull with quick release and hooded levers
Chain Set:	Double chain wheel—49 and 52 tooth—with Stronglight Competition steel cranks
Pedals:	Lyotard with Christophe toe clips and Lapize slip
Gear:	Campagnolo Grand-Sport 10-speed with bottom-up levers. Regina rear sprocket—14, 16, 18, 21 or 24 tooth . . . cable operated from shifting lever
Saddle:	Brooks Competition Standard B17

ALL SPECIFICATIONS SUBJECT TO CHANGE WITHOUT NOTICE.

Original Specifications

1963 Schwinn Paramount

Weight: 22.5 lbs
Price: $175 (new)

Jared Fisher's Ride 2021

San Diego, California, to St. Augustine, Florida
2900 miles in 16 days.
Price: $4,500 (new)

TECHNICAL DIFFERENCES

Old School vs. New School

Road Bike Ten-Speed

- Five-Speed Rear Cluster 14–28

- Two-Speed Front Chain Rings 47–52

- Reynolds 531 Steel Tube Frame

- Sew-Up Tires–Need a Pump

Gravel Bike

- Specialized Diverge

- Twenty-Two Gears

- Weight 55 lbs, as Seen

- Equipped with Tools, Ground Pad, Down Sleeping Bag, Charging System for Cell Phone, Drone, and Lights.

- Extra Sealent for Tubeless Tires

- Notice No Clipless Pedals on Jared's Bike, Flats Only.

We would have done a lot less walking if we had the mountain bike. The mountain bike would have been able to carry more equipment. Maybe a tent. We would have waited another fifty years for the mountain bike evolution. There were no mountain bikes in 1965.

Norm Hansen, Bruce Schwab, and Parker Hansen

Bruce Schwab sent the bike to the Schwinn Waterford Factory in Wisconsin and the bike was restored to 98 percent of its original condition.

ALL TOGETHER, PUSH — Bicyclists Norman Hansen (left) and Richard Frick are going to leave the Harbor Area this way Saturday. They hope to arrive at the New York World's Fair in six weeks.

MAP OF CALIFORNIA

1965

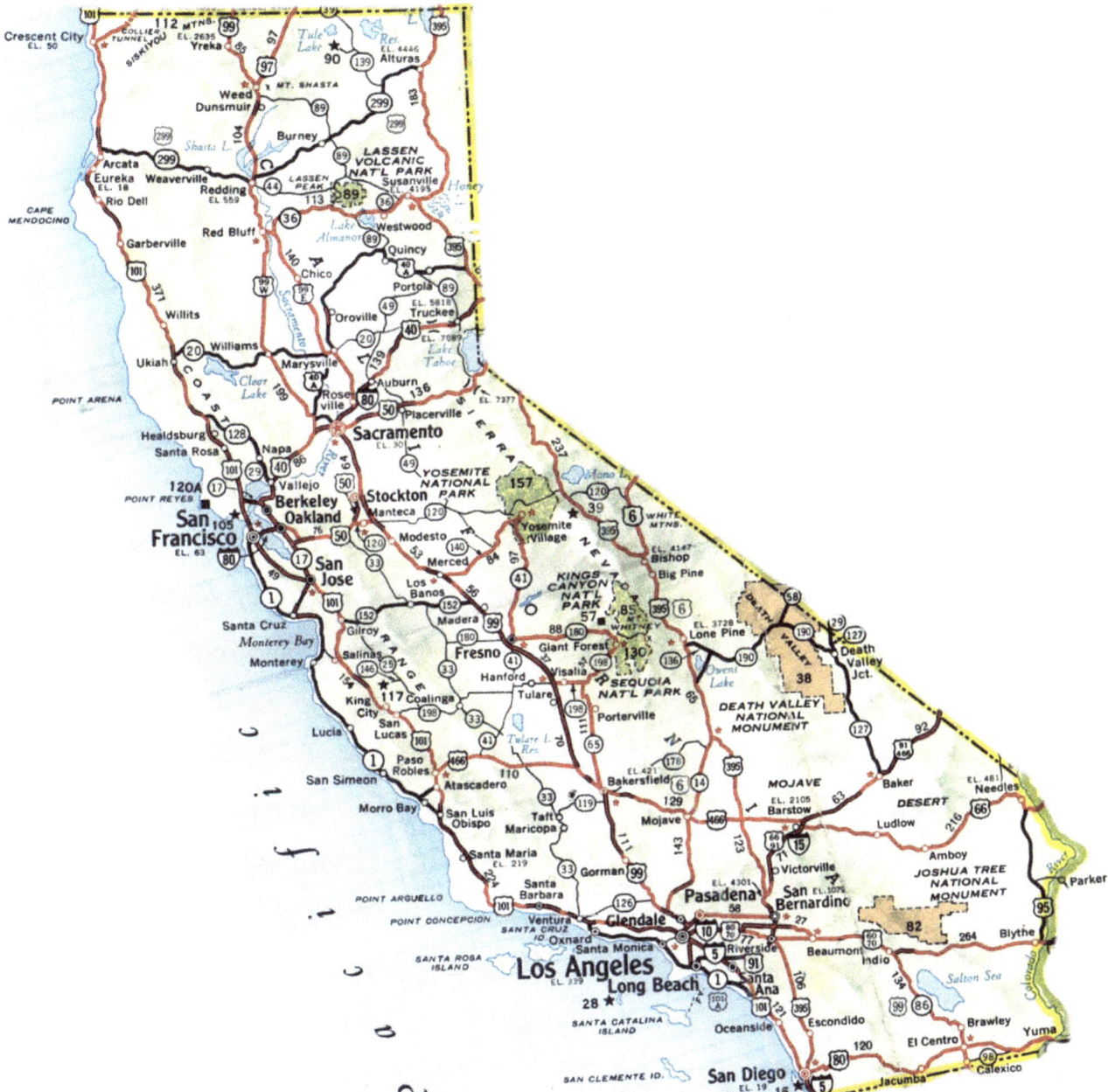

Pedal, Pedal, Pedal

Harbor Youths Plan Six-week Marathon

By EVELYN SHERWOOD
Of the Daily Pilot Staff

Two Harbor Area youths today are planning tp pedal their way clear out of town.

And pedal, and pedal, and pedal — nearly 3,500 miles to the New York World's Fair.

The intrepid bicylists are students Richard Frick, 19, of 124 45th St., Newport Beach; and Norman Hansen, 21, of 2512 College Place, Costa Mesa.

They plan to start their trip on leg-powered two-wheelers Saturday at 9 a.m.

If all goes well, within the next six weeks, they will have pedaled through Blythe, past Amarillo, Texas, across the Kansas plains, through the metropoli of Chicago and Newark, N.J., and be in sight of the big steel globe at the World's Fair.

Hansen, an Orange Coast College student, figured awhile back that he needed to get in shape for pedaling to New York.

So he took a tuneup ride t Seattle.

Frick, a February graduate from Newport Harbor High School, on the other hand hasn't had any long distance bicycling experience.

He figures he'll be in pretty fair shape when he arrives in New York. "I'll practice on the way," he explains.

Both youths will ride 10-speed Italian Bianchi bicycles. They'll carry spare tires and sleeping bags with them.

Friends will gather Saturday morning at the Park Lido Homes parking lot to toast the lads with coffee cups as they pedal off into the early morning mists.

"This is going to be a real hard trip," Hansen bubbled in enthusiasm today. "It's going to be a trial of endurance."

Some people figure he didn't really need to explain that.

DAY 1

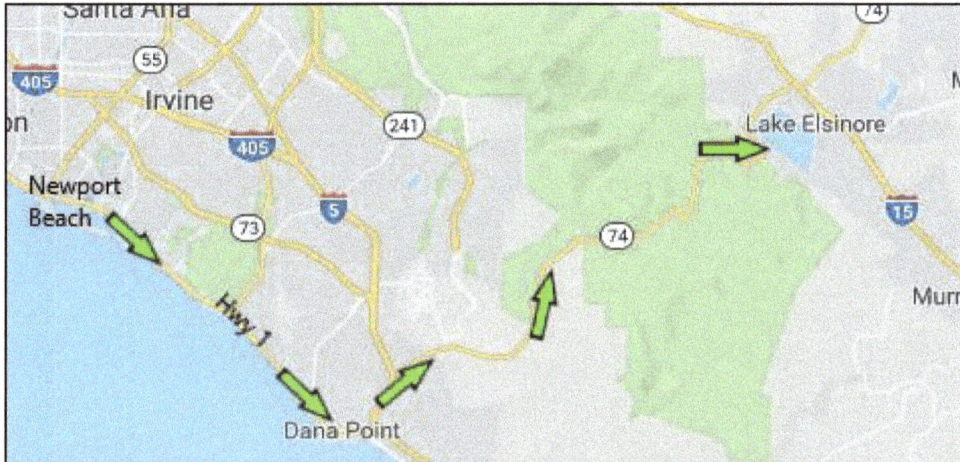

Newport Beach, California, to Elsinore, California

58 Miles

We departed Saturday, May 1, 1965, from Newport Beach, California, at 9:00 a.m. We rode over the top of the notoriously accident-prone Ortega Pass to Lake Elsinore.

I rode by myself for the last two hours. Poor old Butch had to get off and walk. I guess the hill was too much, but he did really well for the first day considering his shape.

People were very friendly when they saw the "Newport Beach, CA" patches on the backs of our jackets. They may have heard about us taking this trip. We got a free cup of coffee and cookies at a campground we stopped at, and that's the way it would be all across America—kindness, generosity, and questions.

We spent the night at Butch's grandparents in Lake Elsinore and slept great! We were going to try and make it to "Indio" the next day. It was approximately fifty-six miles—mostly mountains—and a 2,600-feet altitude climb.

Picture of Lake Elsinore in 1965

DAY 2

SUNDAY, MAY 2

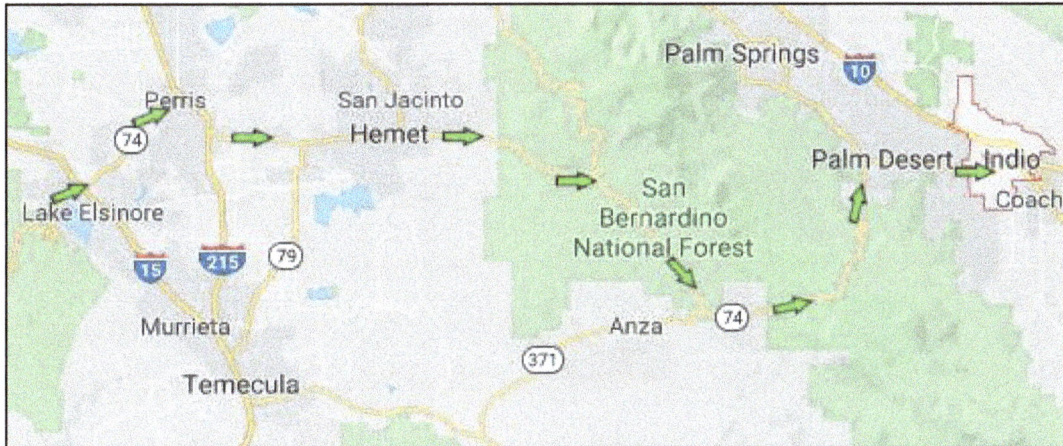

Elsinore, California, to Indio, California
100 Miles

Elsinore to Indio meant going over Hemet Pass at an altitude of approximately 6,800 feet. We left Elsinore at daybreak, and instead of the 6,800-foot Hemet Pass, we took a detour suggested by some locals we met. Rather than an easier ride, we had a frightening experience descending down the Eleven Mile Grade into Palm Desert. We arrived in Indio at 6:30 p.m.

The wind was with us, blowing at sixty miles an hour, and we hit speeds of nearly fifty miles an hour. We rounded a sharp curve and were nearly blown off the mountain and down a three-hundred-foot drop. *Wow!*

One danger with this type of trip was getting hurt. The doctor told us that if either one of us fell, we would not be able to ride. We decided not to draft each other in order to eliminate an accident. Staying a good distance apart helped us avoid potholes and debris on the road. There were no shoulders so staying on the asphalt road was very important in not falling.

2 Bicyclists Past Blythe

The Harbor Area's two marathon bicyclists h a v e pedaled past Blythe and are headed for Phoenix, Arizona, as their next major stop on the way to the New York World's Fair, it was reported today.

The long distance riders are Norman Hansen, 21, of 2512 N. Colby Place, Costa Mesa, and Richard Frick, 19, of 124 45th St., Newport Beach. They left on their cross-continent ride Saturday.

Hansen's mother, Mrs. Mason Johnson, said she had received a telephone report that the boys are "doing well" and still pedaling away strongly.

Scared the hell out of both of us, but we arrived unscathed in Indio. Butch was making gains and did a lot better that day.

These are the telescopes above Lake Elsinore, California.

DAY 3

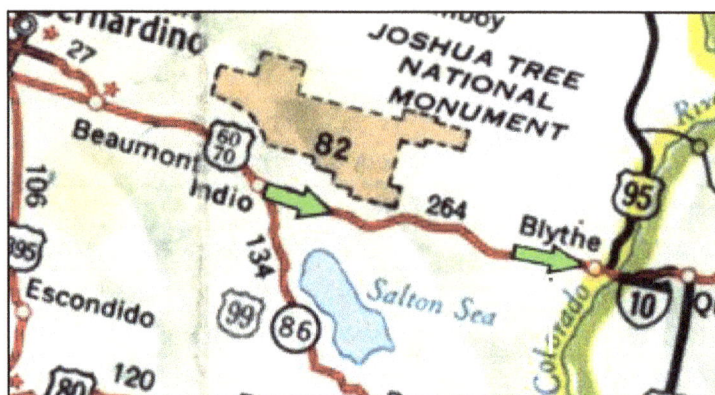

Indio, California, to Blyth, California
100 Miles

We woke up the next morning in Indio, California. Slept with the wind howling all night and sand blowing everywhere. Everything was full of sand. Even my eyelids were sandy. Near Blyth, I had to put on long pants. Got too sunburned— remember, we had no sunblock in those days.

A determination was pushing me on more than physical force. I found myself salting soup, salads, everything, without realizing it. I think our bodies responded with impulses to the brain without conscious thought. This could have been the start of fatigue or electrolyte depletion.

We stopped at the Travel Lodge in Blyth, where I took my first bath in two days in the pool that night. We rode over one hundred miles the day before.

My body was starting to hurt—sunburn, water shortage, and peanut butter sandwiches on white bread were getting old! No power bars, no Gatorade. We got water from people on the highway in those canvas bags they hung on the bumpers. These canvas bags were for cars with overheating radiators in the desert heat. We never anticipated a water shortage since we had no idea how desolate it is across Arizona and New Mexico. The cars would always stop and see if we needed anything! We really needed the help from all the cars that came by.

Canvas Water Bag, 1965

MAP OF ARIZONA

1965

Glendale
GRAND CANYON NATIONAL MONUMENT
118
Jacob Lake
Marble Canyon
GLEN CANYON DAM
MONUMENT VALLEY PK.
107
Kayenta
Shiprock
64
Davis
17
Chinle
64
GRAND CANYON NAT'L PARK
65
64
HOOVER DAM
87
LAKE MEAD NAT'L RECREATION AREA
Grand Canyon
Cameron
57
89
155
Moenkopi
264
Oraibi
Window Rock
264
St. Michaels
HUMPHREYS PEAK
137
DAVIS DAM
102
114
Williams
66
20
36
59
180
64
87
66
180
Winslow
Sanders
96
789
Kingman EL. 3325
Ash Fork
Flagstaff
148
Holbrook EL. 5075
116
89
17
144
Jerome
Clarkdale
99
180
93
St. Johns
666
Prescott EL. 5280
93
153
79
Camp Verde
Pine
77
Show Low
789
69
136
87
Springerville EL. 6965
115
ARIZONA
Roosevelt Lake
177
Alpine
Parker
89
69
Wickenburg EL. 2093
Roosevelt
60
666
95
72
71
51
EL. 1092
140
88
88
Miami
EL. 3541
Globe
San Carlos Lake
60
60
70
Salome
69
Phoenix
Quartzsite
Buckeye
80
Mesa
50
789
Gila River
70
Clifton
10
65
87
93
287
Florence
82
193
Gila Bend EL. 735
Casa Grande
22
Safford
Yuma
8
80
84
128
125
80
89
666
Duncan
95
176
85
10
84
93
Tucson EL. 2372
Willcox
160
San Luis
95
ORGAN PIPE CACTUS NATIONAL MONUMENT
Ajo
124A
124
86
Cochise
30
113
86
181
Rodeo
8
Sonoita
789
Benson
Tombstone
86
666 EL. 5490
Bisbee
80
89
142
82
220
249
32A
92
Nogales
Douglas

II

HIGHWAY BRIDGE
Salt River Canyon, Arizona
The traveler following U.S. Highway 60 between Globe and Show Low, Arizona, crosses this graceful structure deep in the colorful Salt River Canyon. Below the bridge and along the river are picnic tables and shelters for tourists.

Petley

5c U.S. POSTAGE

Published by Petley Studios, 4051 E. Van Buren, Phoenix, Arizona

Color Photo by Bob Petley
Plastichrome®

P36939

We did 91 Miles Today,
75% up hill with an 8% grade to 1,000 feet.
It's 35° here in Show Low
Arizona. we will be
in New Mexico Sunday
May 9 - Thats Tommarrow.
We know you and Ter
where out Tosee usan
the other side of Blyth.
you missed us. Please
send all important Letters
or information To Elec's in
Amarillo, Texas.
50 E + Grand
Dewey Webb. NORM.

POST CARD

MASON + Evelyn
Johnson
2512 Colby Place.
Costa Mesa,
California.

DAY 4

SANDWICH FIGHT

Blythe to Quartzsite, Arizona, to Salome, Arizona

60 Miles

Quartzsite is a ghost town. It was a stagecoach stop back in the day. It had a population of twenty-five people, but was "increasing" in 1965, according to a lady sitting in a dirty old cafe next to another 350-plus-pound, red-headed lady. Some mean-looking people lived out there in the desert.

An old man was sitting next to me with brown broken fingers and the dirtiest fingernails I'd ever seen. He had long, greasy hair and reddish-brown eyes. Who was he? He had a knapsack between his legs. I had never seen a dirtier human than this guy. His fingernails were bent over the ends of the bone, as if someone put each of his fingers in a vise and bent them over as you would with a nail in a board. What a frightful human being. A drunken Negro stumbled in and sat down. We had never seen people like this. Before I could say anything to Butch, he had ordered cheeseburgers, since we were both starving for calories. We slept in Arizona somewhere on the ground. Also rode another sixty miles that day.

I got up the next morning and noticed my sandwiches were gone out of my black bike bag. I accused Butch of taking them. Since we were so hungry, we never shared our sandwiches. We learned that sleeping in the desert needed experience. Back then, people would camp along the side of the road and burn their tin cans and garbage in the fire. The local rodents would come after dark and rummage through the campfire.

After looking around, we found the cellophane wrappers without the sandwiches. A local rodent wormed his way into my bag and hauled them off. From then on, we looked around for high ground with no campfire remains. No more waiting until nearly dark to find a place to sleep on the ground!

DAY 5

THE DESERT

Salome, Arizona, to Phoenix, Arizona

108 Miles

Trying to find a café was not easy since fast-food chains were just getting started. We ate at Pettigrew's Restaurant. We slept in the pool dressing room somewhere in a Salome, Arizona, park. Pettigrew's was a good restaurant, but we had to get to Phoenix the next day.

We were sitting in a laundromat, waiting for our clothes to dry. I had broken a spoke on the rear wheel. I was in a very depressed mood thinking about my future. Butch talked too much and was too apprehensive—unlike me, with no fear of anything. Maybe if I had some fear, I would not be doing this trip. I didn't have much time to write, as I was too busy riding, and besides, without the flashlight—long since broken and discarded—writing at night was difficult. There were no LED bulbs as they have today. We all seem to be in such a hurry these days. Maybe that's what the hereafter will be . . . a timeless life.

2 Bicyclists Now Near New Mexico

Harbor Area marathon bicyclists Norman Hansen and Richard Frick, headed for the New York World's Fair, had almost pedaled their way across two states today.

Hansen's mother, Mrs. Mason Johnson, received word today that the two long-distance riders are nearing the Arizona-New Mexico state line.

"They are getting sunburned and weary, but they're pleased with their progress," Mrs. Johnson reported. She said the two distance riders have been staying overnight at the most plush motels. "They stay in their sleeping bags on the lawns," she explained.

Hansen, 21, of 2512 Colby Place, Costa Mesa, and Frick, 19, of 127 45th St., Newport Beach, left Newport April 31 headed for the World's Fair on their foreign racing bikes.

Their next major "rest up" stop is scheduled at Amarillo, Texas.

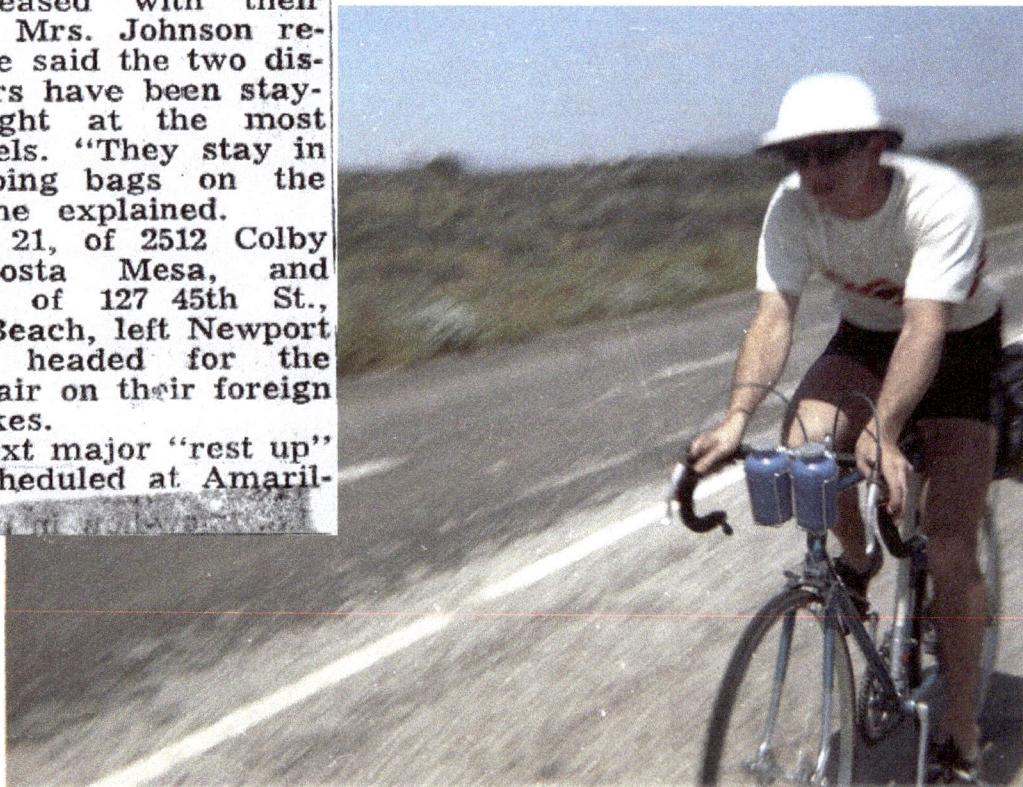

"White Hat"
120 degrees during the daytime.

"Jackets"
Thirty-five degrees at night and freezing.

DAY 6

REST AND REPAIR

There was no riding that. It was a rest day with maintenance on the bikes, oil chains, and Truing Wheels, plus we tightened the derailer cables. We were very tired and losing weight, but we had to go from Phoenix, Arizona, to Superior the next day. We laid by a pool in the sun, with good desert weather. Hot and dry for the elderly. We had to buy new T-shirts to replace the ones Butch ruined in the washer. Dumbass washed whites with the colored pants, and the result was blue T-shirts, and he decided to dry them on high. Now, they were shrunk too! He was starting to annoy me nearly as much as the rear wheel rubbing against the brake pad!

We met two colored kids in Phoenix. Samuel, one of the colored kids we met, came from a family of twelve. His father left his mother, married another woman, and was having more kids. We had the same problems in Compton, California—the poor progressing slowly from one generation to another generation. Mixed race marriages in the future!

Samuel said he deliberately worked slowly so he, as he puts it, "won't work himself out of a job." "I ain't gonna find myself working for somebody else to get them rich." My conscience was bothering me—What the hell am I doing out here in the desert, hot, sunburned, fatigued, and sleeping in dirty sleeping bags?

DAY 7

Phoenix, Arizona, to Globe, Arizona
57 Miles

We left Phoenix, Arizona, and arrived in Superior. We passed the Superstition Mountains, and talked to a man who said over fifty people were lost, died, or murdered there in search of legendary lost gold. Now, we were in Indian country, "Apache." You really had to be rugged to live in the desert one hundred years ago.

We slept in the Globe, Arizona, Police Station. We got to sleep on jail cell beds that were a welcome sight and better than the dirty sleeping bags. The police were good guys.

We ate at the Globe Café. A dollar and sixty-five cents for a steak dinner—we each had 125 dollars. Credit cards you say? We didn't need or have credit cards, nor did I ever have a health insurance card!

We met Nina Cochran, twelve-year-old at the café. Who was she? The kids then hung out at the café, hoping someone would play their favorite song on the jukebox. So, I picked a couple of songs and let Nina pick one. Kids were always, curious about our bikes; we always took the time to explain how they worked.

DAY 8

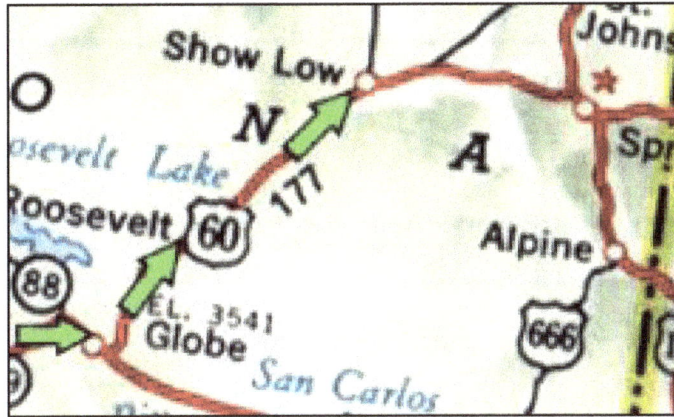

Globe, Arizona, to Show Low, Arizona
Elevation: 6300 feet, 8 percent grade
80 Miles

We stopped by the Salt River Canyon on the Fort Apache Reservation. Salt River divides two reservations. There were green forests, and they were not dense.

The people in these towns seem relaxed, not in any hurry. Globe was this way—slow talking, much different than big cities. They know their own environment very well. The time in the journal said two o'clock. We went up a six-mile grade and had a tough time pulling the grade (8 percent). *Hey, Butch, I hear some semi-trucks coming up behind us—get ready, we need some help.*

We both sprinted to grab hold. Butch missed and could not catch the truck. I caught the truck and was holding onto the rear-gate hinge. I looked up and I saw the ass of a sheep pushing through the wood slats. The driver was pissed. He kept waving in the mirror for me to get off.

"Fuck you, I'm not letting go until the sheep start to shit in front of my wheels."

What a smell. Butch caught a sheep truck and went flying by. I had to let go—too much sheep shit.

Show Low, Arizona, 6,333 feet, thirty-five degrees cold, and do I stink! We were trying to find a place to sleep—of course, on the ground!

MAP OF NEW MEXICO

1965

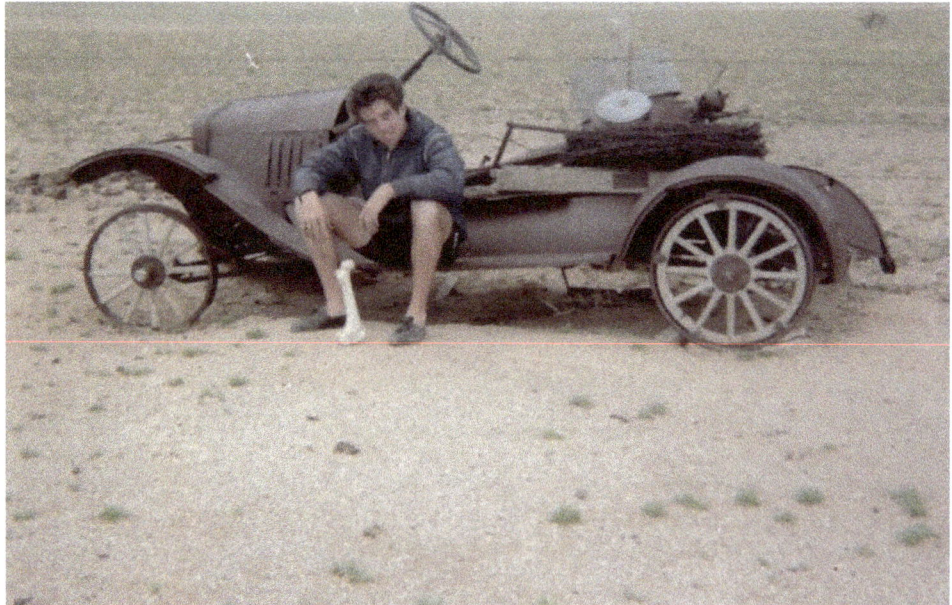

DAY 9

Show Low, Arizona, to Quemado, New Mexico
100 Miles

We entered New Mexico, with bad roads and no shoulder at all. Since we were deep into the desert, we tried riding at night—big mistake. It was very hilly, and had too many potholes. I was so very tired. The lack of calories was taking its toll on us. Peanut butter and jelly sandwiches weren't cutting it. There was nothing between the two stops except a town called Red Hill, a gas station, café, and motel with trailer-type rooms. The first room had a note on a made bed: "I'm sick and had to leave for Albuquerque." An empty abandoned house had old books and a suitcase full of clothes. I kind of had a sick feeling about this town. The night ride was awful. When a car came at us, we were temporarily blinded. As they slowed down, they could not believe what they were seeing. We were two idiots riding at night in the desert with no lights. These were the things we do at this age—stupid things!

We will try to make Socorro, New Mexico, tomorrow in 108 miles.

DAY 10

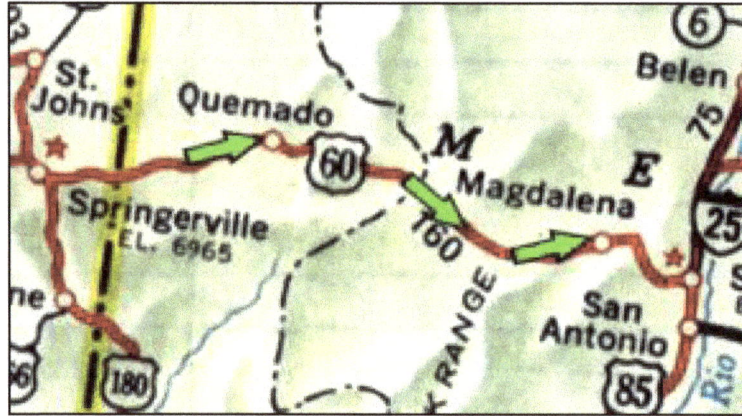

Quemado, New Mexico, to Magdalena, New Mexico
80 Miles

A trip like this widens your scope of life. I had no idea that our country was this big. Ten days on the road and we were still in the desert!

We had a great idea: we thought to sleep in a pull-behind metal trailer off the ground with dual wheels. The tongue of the trailer was tipped down, so we leveled it. Another stupid idea!

Born intelligence versus acquired intelligence; apparently neither of us had either! We hardly slept at all, with the winds blowing over and under us. We found out the next day it was fourteen degrees that night.

Everything was frozen—sleeping bags, shoes, even my journal had frost on it. We damn near froze to death. Remember: too early for down jackets or down sleeping bags. Butch kept asking "Why are you writing in that damn book? You can, hardly see at night." He was right.

DAY 11

Socorro, New Mexico, to Mountainair, New Mexico

Mining Town—4,600 feet—very tired. Butch did not look good. Neither did I! I was very frightened. There weren't any doctors, no hospitals, no ambulance, no helicopters as they have today. If one of us got hurt, we were in real trouble. We decided not to shift gears much since we have only one wire cable between us for the derailleurs. If the wire broke, we had none left. At the Socorro School of Mining, we met an old man who had a shoe repair shop. Our shoes were falling apart since we sometimes had to get off and walk.

His shop was on Grant Street. There was only one type of biking shoe at the time and they were uncomfortable to walk in with a metal cleat attached to the sole. The metal cleats under the soles fit in our mousetrap pedals. We only had tennis shoes; we should have been wearing them more often.

See the following picture of my bike shoe, with my foot hanging out since they were broken.

The shoe repair guy told us the street was called Hangman's Street back in the '20s. They would hang people on the cottonwood trees at night and they would be there in the morning for all to see. He showed us pictures—yuck. They were usually Negroes, Indians, and Chinese. The town, back then during the mining boom, was twenty to thirty thousand people. We were onto Encino,

New Mexico, the next day. Public executions were considered a deterrent against criminal behavior.

We left Socorro, New Mexico, for Mountainair, New Mexico. A guy named Phil Sanders stopped us and invited us to this "job core" camp. It was designed for poor teenagers from inner cities. I think they called it "The War on Poverty Crusade." There must have been one hundred teenagers. Hell, they were our age. All fascinated with our bikes. One kid said, "One hundred and seventy-five dollars for a bike? Hell, I could buy a car for that." Mostly were colored kids, Mexican kids, and a few white kids. We had dinner in the mess hall and slept in bunk beds. What a relief. No rocks to move under the bag. We had breakfast and left early the next morning.

The Grapes of Wrath *Car*

I was walking down a street in Encino, New Mexico, in 1965.
I called it a town but it was called, back then, a village.

DAY 12

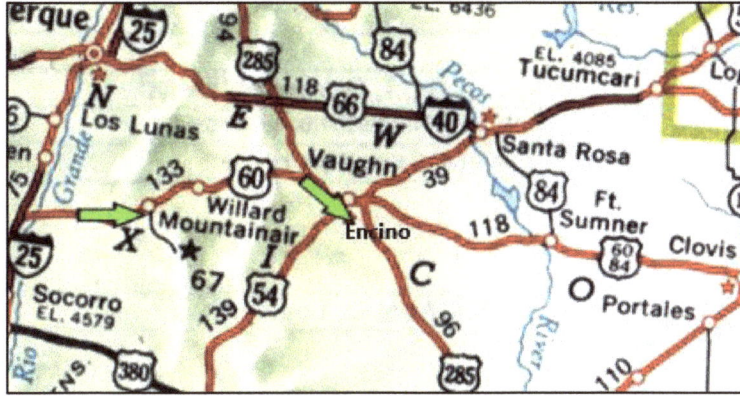

Mountainair, New Mexico, to Encino, New Mexico

110 Miles

We made it to Encino, New Mexico, and had lunch there, near Encino High School—fifty-six students, six cheerleaders in the restaurant. The girls looked at our Newport Beach patches and asked us if we surfed. That's when the lying started. Of course, neither one of us surfed, although we had tried. We were not worth a crap on a surfboard.

We stopped along the road and met a guy named Tommy Hamilton. He was on a horse and the horse was afraid of the bikes. In fact, even Tommy had never seen bikes like these. He was about seventy years old and told us he had drilled water wells for the railroad when they were laying tracks. Tommy came from Germany in 1902. Interesting guy.

Butch looked really tired—headache and fatigue! I couldn't see myself, but I probably looked worse. I wasn't sure if we could do this, but I never would say that to Butch. We hated to leave Encino, New Mexico, since we had not seen any pretty girls in two weeks. I was smelly, unshaven. We both looked bad. Forgot about it, got back on our bikes, and started again.

1243A PDT MAY 14 65 QB016

DA541 D AMAQ06 NL PD CS CLOVIS NMEX 13

POPS BIKE SHOP

  118 SOUTH MAIN SANTA ANA CALIF

SEND FOUR SEW-UP TIRES TO AMARILLO TEXAS TO REACH THERE
SATURDAY. MUST HAVE BY SATURDAY MAY 15. SEND TO POST OFFICE
IN AMARILLO TEXAS ALSO MY TIRES AND TUBES BOTH BLEW. WILL SEND
BACK SPECIMEN OF DEFAULT. WE ARE STRANDED IN CLOVIS N. MEXICO
WILL WAIT FOR REPLY IN AMARILLO THOUGH

     NORM

DAY 13

THURSDAY, MAY 13

BIKE FAILURE!

Encino, New Mexico, to Clovis, New Mexico

75 Miles

We had sent a telegram on May 5 from Phoenix, Arizona, telling everyone we would make it to Amarillo, Texas, on May 15.

We would rest for a day, make bike repairs, etc.

Well, both tires and tube blew out so bad that the tube could not be patched, and I was out of spare tubes. The bike with sew-ups had been holding up better than the bike with standard tubes and tires.

Tube repair on sew-up tires was tedious and time-consuming. The Velox repair kit had needles, thread, and a thimble to repair the inner liner. See the original repair kit, with glue included. I used it once, and from there on, I sent the telegrams for new sew-ups.

Anyway, we were stranded, ended about twenty-five miles from Clovis, New Mexico. After what seemed like hours, we finally flagged down a guy in a pick-up truck. He agreed to haul us to Clovis. We got to a Firestone store that had tires and tubes. I was very lucky. The guy in the truck had never seen these types of bikes.

Thanks to the firemen, we ended up sleeping in the back of a fire station in Clovis, New Mexico. We got great food from some place and planned to leave early in morning to try and make it to Amarillo, Texas.

Firestone sign store

MAP OF TEXAS

1965

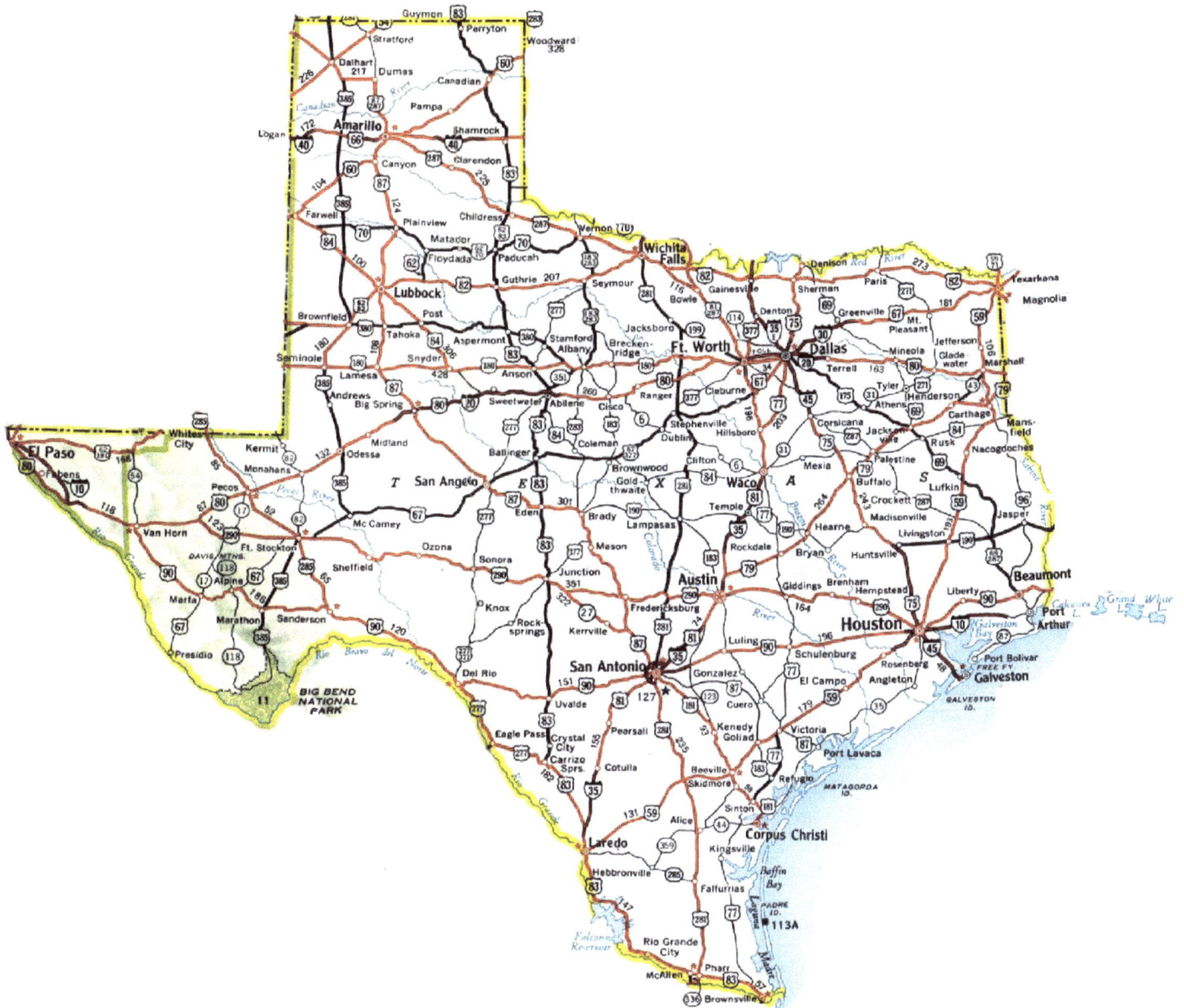

DAY 14

Clovis, New Mexico, to Amarillo, Texas

115 Miles

What a day! We rode 115 miles, in approximately six hours. We had a fifty mph wind to our back. We rode continuously with only two stops.

Six blocks from our destination at Aunt Elsie and Uncle Dewey's, we had another blowout. This time we were near a gas station—free air, no hand pumps.

We made it to Aunt Elsie and Uncle Dewey's house. We could finally rest and make our bike repairs.

DAY 15

REST DAY!

Amarillo, Texas

Uncle Dewey had a southern drawl; it was interesting listening to him. They were both in their sixties and retired. The Civil Rights Movement was on and I was curious about his views on the racial issue.

I will quote what he said as I wrote it in my journal: "I believe in integration, I believe in complete freedom for the Negroes, I think there will be interracial marriages." He also thought the space program was a big waste of time and money. "We need to spend on our planet, not the ones out there." It was 1965 and he may have been correct about predicting climate change.

Teenagers in Texas seemed to enjoy a different type of living. It seemed cleaner here, unlike Los Angeles with its smog and trash. People would leave their beer bottles and trash on the beach there. This was prior to the litterbug program. In 1953, Vermont passed a law banning "throw away bottles." Fines were levied for littering. So a slogan, "Don't Be a Litterbug," became a popular advertisement. The object was to keep America beautiful. Not many waste

BIKE ACROSS AMERICA 1965

management programs had been implemented at that time. In fact, Huntington Beach, California, was named "Tin Can Beach" back in 1960. People even lived there year around. In the morning, we planned to leave. We called home and were told of all the news articles and publicity we were getting. Since we had been unaware of that information, it gave us more incentive to finish the trip.

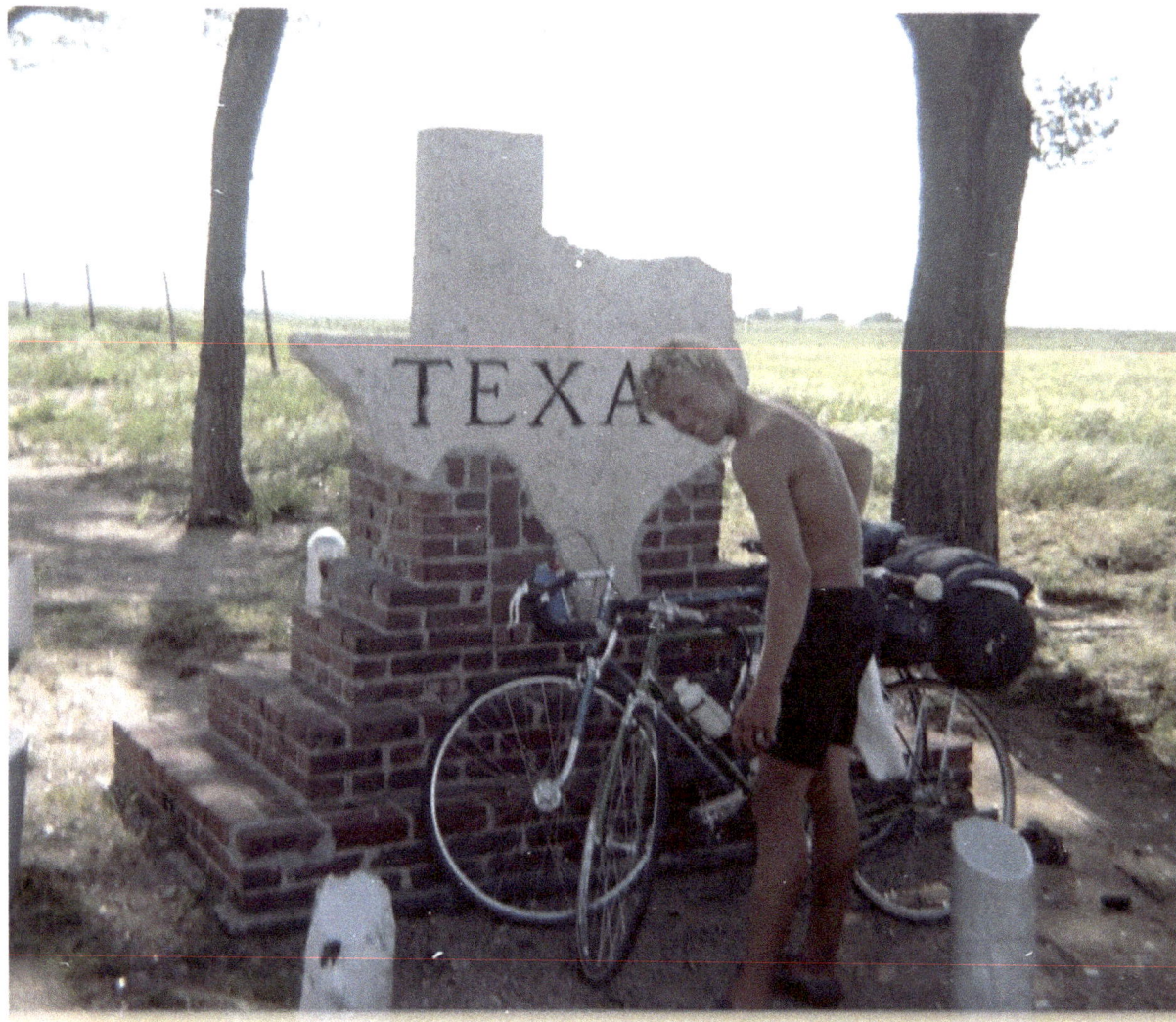

DAY 16

Amarillo, Texas, to Pampa, Texas
56 Miles

We made it to Pampa, Texas, with no major problems. The geography was changing, flat but not scorching heat, as it was in the desert. I was just trying to get back in the rhythm and start without the pain.

We encountered two terrible odors. One of the worst was a manure farm—hundreds of steers all bunched together, eating and shitting while waiting to go to the slaughterhouse. The wind was blowing at our backs and we were almost unable to breathe.

The second was about twenty miles down the road—oil and gas refinery—a chemical smell. This was the first time we wished the wind was not at our back.

It was 1:30 in the afternoon, and we were sitting in a park thinking of the days' ride. We played baseball with an old pro who was throwing batting practice.

I told him we were from California and were state baseball champs in 1962. He waved me to the plate. Amazingly, I hit the ball—a line drive. If only I had speed. Anyway, thirteen years I wasted playing baseball!

Butch hand-pumping up tires; leaving Amarillo, Texas, for Pampa, Texas.

MAP OF OKLAHOMA

1965

DAY 17

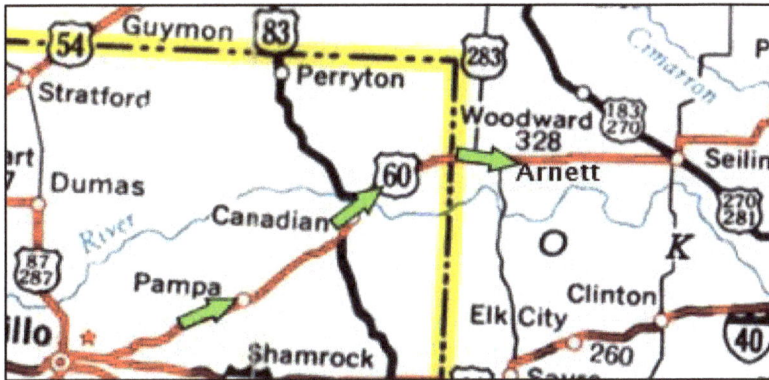

Pampa, Texas, to Arnett, Oklahoma
86 Miles

We left Pampa at 10 a.m. and arrived in Arnett, Oklahoma, at 5:30 p.m. We listened to Okie music in Oklahoma, at an LL gas station, while watching a fat man wearing suspenders and a huge cowboy hat. I was sitting, staring out the window. When I looked at his face, he was toothless, with his gums and lips sunk back at least three inches. He would stick his tongue up his nostrils. He looked at me and said, "Betcha can't do this." YUCK! The things you see when you are younger. We never saw this in Newport Beach.

The geography was changing yet again. We were now passing large fields of green grass or wheat, or something.

We went through Norman, Oklahoma.

The weather was cooler and the roads were not as awful as in the first thousand miles. No, we were not getting any stronger; we were just trying to manage one painful day after the next!

Welcome to Oklahoma.

Typical bridge of the day!

Miss Sharron Frick.
1975 Pomona Ave.
Costa Mesa, California

92660

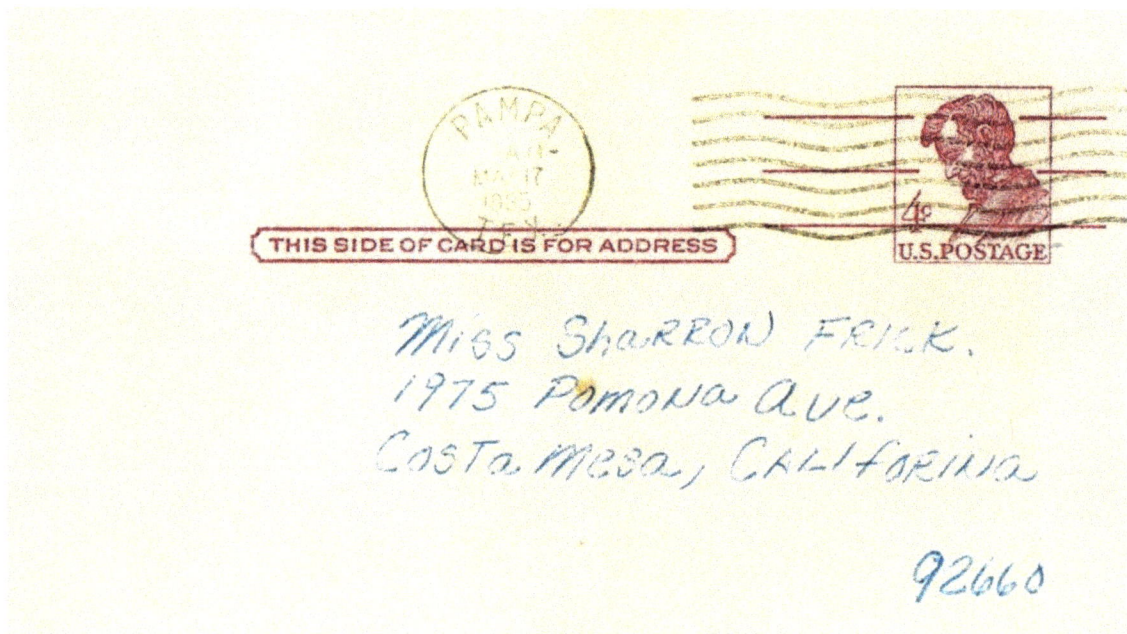

*Butch sent this post card to his sister and he would send
our rolls of film to her for developing.*

WELL I RECEIVED YOUR LETTER AT MR. & MRS. WEBB AND WAS HAPPY TO HEAR FROM YA, AL THE WEATHER IS FINE NOW & AM GLAD TO HEAR YOUR KEEPING A SCRAP BOOK, I SENT FOUR ROLLS OF FILM TO ST. LOUIS TO BE PICKED UP AFTER DEVELOPING I HOPE BOB GETS HOME EARLY & TELL THE MEM AT WORK I AM DOIN FINE IN FACT IAM DOIN BETTER THEN NORM (I KEEP GOING & TIRS HIM OUT & ME 2 BUT I KEEP PUSHING ON). I HAVENT SEEN NO GIRLS SO DON'T WORRY ABOUT THAT (NO TIME) WELL I AM GOING TO DROP MARKY A LINE SEE YA SOON BUTCH.

Butch starts to get competitive.

DAY 18

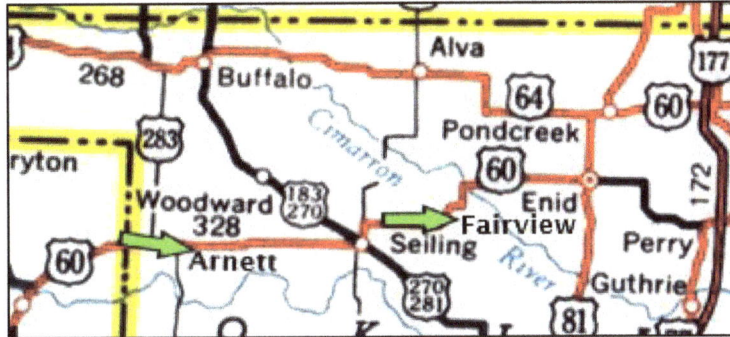

Arnett, Oklahoma, to Fairview, Oklahoma

80 Miles

We left Arnett at eight a.m. We saw a lot of flowers along the highway. Butch and I had a twenty-mile race to help with boredom. I won but really had to strain myself. For the first time, I saw hate for me in his eyes. Was something eating at him?

The road was better but still had no shoulder. I thought you could run away from problems, and that's what I was doing. I wondered if it would work?

Here in the central US, the people are used to four seasons—and they seem happy about that—unlike southern California which has one season. Families looked forward to the seasonal changes. At least that's what we heard when we talked to the locals. It was very sticky and humid but did feel better than the hot desert heat.

Now, more cars were stopping alongside and offering us cookies, cokes, and candy bars. Hell, we ate anything they gave us. I was so sick of peanut butter sandwiches! The women always wanted to take our pictures. So we would hold onto the car door handles one at a time. Kind of fun!

MAP OF KANSAS

1965

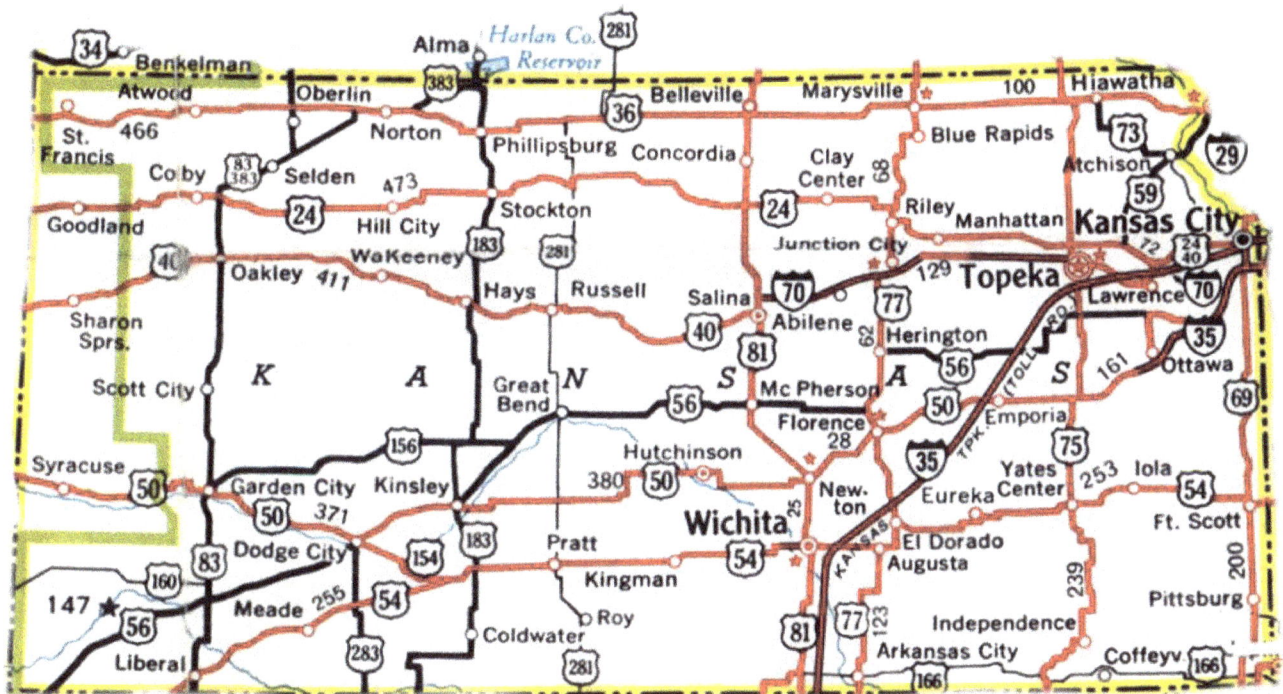

Bicyclists Welcomed In Kansas

Harbor Area marathon bicyclists Norman Hansen and Richard "Butch" Frick won a rousing welcome in Kansas this week as they pedaled their way through the Sunflower State toward the New York World's Fair.

Hansen, 21, of 2512 Colby Place, Costa Mesa, and Frick, 19, of 127 45th St., Newport Beach, pedaled in one day from Fairview, Okla., to Caldwell, Kans., where they were interviewed by The Caldwell Messenger of Sumner County.

The youths told the newspaper that so far they've gone through 10 bike tires and been run off the road by motorists several times during their cross-continent ride.

Hansen also split his riding pants on a particularly rough segment of the trip.

In Caldwell, Hansen and Frick slept overnight in city jail because of the threat of rain. Later they were interviewed on the 10 o'clock news in Wichita, Kans. They left Newport Aug. 11 and are due in St. Louis, Mo., Monday.

DAY 19

HERE COME THE DOGS

Fairview, Oklahoma, to Caldwell, Kansas

100 Miles

Remember, this *is* 1965, way before the leash laws came into effect. Every farm we could see in the distance had dogs. Usually two or three! We could see them running toward us, thinking, "Look! Fresh white meat."

During the first couple of attacks, we would hit them over the head with our tire pumps. After one of the pumps got a dent in it, we realized we could break our pumps and would have no air with constant flats! So, we decided to ride side by side and hit them on the end of their nose. A bit of yelping was heard, but it worked. No dog bites! There weren't many dogs the first eight hundred miles. It was too hot in the desert for chasing bikes and cars.

We left Fairview after being invited to a cook's house to stay overnight. We met the cook at the restaurant where we had stopped to eat.

Butch felt sorry for the guy, so we accepted. He was a very lonely man who had been a cook for over thirty years and had no future. To this day, I can remember how happy he was that he had company at his apartment. He was fat, balding, wore glasses, and had lost most of his teeth. He had never been married. We told him wild stories about women in bikinis on the beach in Newport. A lot of guys just like him would have enjoyed that!

While going from Fairview, Oklahoma, to Caldwell, Kansas, Butch and I stopped and had our picture taken at the Kansas Historical Marker.

Talk about Kansas wheat.

DAY 20

THURSDAY, MAY 20

Caldwell, Kansas, to Wichita, Kansas

65 Miles

We slept as guests in the Caldwell, Kansas, jail. There were no other inmates so we had both cells to ourselves with one cop on duty that night.

We were interviewed for the local TV network, Channel 12, for the ten o'clock news. There were only three networks back then—ABC, CBS, and NBC. Color TV did not start until 1966, so all the TVs were black and white.

They always asked the same question: "Why are you guys doing this?" At our age, not much thought went into anything. If I had thought much about it, I probably would not have done the trip.

We were standing up—neither of us knew the difference between tall wheat and tall grass! We were just a couple of dumbasses from the beach.

A guy named Rick D'Aura said he made a similar trip from San Diego, California, to Miami, Florida, but stated, "I did not have these kinds of bikes." On our way from Wichita, Kansas, to El Dorado, Kansas, we stopped and sent another telegram.

Coast To Coast By Bicycle Not Easy To Do

Butch Frick, 19, and Norman Hansen, 21, of Newport Beach California, spent Wednesday night in Caldwell. The two young men are on a coast to coast bicycle trip from Newport Beach to the World's Fair in New York.

They left California 19 days ago; however, they have only been travling 16 days as they rested at Phoenix and Amarillo. They came here from Fairview, Okla., Wednesday. They peddle from 90 to 100 miles a day.

They have had some trouble along the way. They are riding English style racing bikes and they said they had 10 tires go out on them, They have been run off the road several times by motorists.

The boys said the first few days were tough on them as they were in the mountains and were not toughened to riding long distances.

Young ████ made the Seattle Fair by bicycle, so this trip is not a new experience for him.

They carry light packs, including sleeping bags, and sleep out during good weather. They thought it was going to rain Wednesday night so they bedded down in the City jail.

The Daily Pilot in Newport Beach is keeping track of the boys as they make their way to the Fair.

Stupid decisions don't take long to make.

WESTERN UNION
TELEGRAM

CLASS OF SERVICE

This is a fast message
unless its deferred char-
acter is indicated by the
proper symbol.

W. P. MARSHALL, PRESIDENT

SF-1201 (4-60)

SYMBOLS

DL=Day Letter

NL=Night Letter

LT=International
Letter Telegram

The filing time shown in the date line on domestic telegrams is LOCAL TIME at point of origin. Time of receipt is LOCAL TIME at point of destination

414P PDT MAY 21 65 0A260 KB433

K WZB310 NL PD AUGUSTA KANS 21

POPS BIKE SHOP

118 SOUTH MAIN SANTA ANA CALIF

SEND TWO SEW UPS RIDING SHORTS SIZE #1 TO STLOUIS POST OFFICE

GENERAL DELIVERY MUST HAVE BY WEDNESDAY MAY 26. SO NO BIG HURRY

SINCE TODAY IS FRIDAY 21ST MADE THE TV STATION IN WICHITA CROTCH

RIPPED OUT OF SHORTS CHAMOIS TOO. CONTACT PARENTS FOR ME AND

THEYLL GIVE EXTRA INFORMATION

NORM

Western Union Telegram

DAY 21

FRIDAY, MAY 21

GAY RIGHTS MOVEMENT

Wichita, Kansas, to El Dorado, Kansas, Highway 50–54
34 Miles

We arrived at El Dorado, Kansas, to more publicity. The radio station, KBT, had a ten-minute tape replay at 5:30 p.m. about our trip.

I guess, since we were from California, people thought we must be queers. A guy came into the gas station, and he wanted to talk with us. I thought he might have a place for us to stay. No, just another "damn queer." In those days, prejudice reigned supreme. Why did everyone think we were homosexuals? In the sixties, Laguna Beach, California, was a gay community. We had no problems with gay guys. There were already gay bars in southern California.

I was getting tired of these insinuations; someone was going to get the shit kicked out of them. In 1962, Illinois outlawed charging gay lifestyles as a criminal offense. Anyway, we were too busy chasing women. Butch felt bad again because I beat him at a game of pool. I tried to beat him as badly as possible because I liked to win. He thought I used him to build my ego, and I did. I was starting to get edgy and I was feeling angry. This was not good; things were starting to boil!

Another rest time after another large hill climb.

DAY 22

BUTCH—BIG FIGHT!

El Dorado, Kansas, to Iola, Kansas
83 Miles

We finished eighty-three miles in flat and beautiful Kansas in what seemed to be either endless wheat fields or grass. We had stored our bikes in an abandoned gas station in the bathrooms.

Butch was a pacifist, very sensitive, and artistic in nature. He was an adopted child and he did not know his father, while I also wanted to find my father. I could never beat the hell out of Butch (it would be like hitting a priest) but it finally happened! We were again in a pool hall. The towns were getting closer together, so we could usually find a place to sleep and a café. In those days, the pool hall was a favorite hangout for bored teenagers. Our weight loss had stabilized by now, so we could eat regularly, but daily riding was wearing on our mental state. Butch really laid into me about constantly beating him at pool. I was already edgy, so I threw the cue on the table and said, "You can ride by yourself tomorrow." With him berating me about the pool game, and people thinking we were a couple of "queers" from California, I was losing it.

We were both scowling at each other when the front door opened and in came a young guy with a lettermen jacket on. He had a flat-top haircut and he looked at us and said, "Where are you two queers from?"

I felt the rage coming on. Another kid standing next to me with black-rimmed glasses said he was a football player and whispered, "Be careful." Butch looked at me and I said, "Head back to the bikes." He knew!

I grew up in Compton, California, in a predominantly Black neighborhood until the age of twelve. I attended Catholic school and had a WWII marine for a stepfather. With raging testosterone, I had all the ingredients for pent-up anger! I thought for a moment about getting arrested and ruining our trip. Rage took over common sense, though. I had enough! I told the kid with the glasses to tell Mr. Flattop I'd meet him in the alley. I picked up a two-by-four and was ready. It was pitch-black out. He came out the door, took one step down, and I hit him across his midsection. He tumbled into the gravel. I stood over him as he was gasping for air and said, "Am I queer now?" I kicked him in the face as he was mumbling something. I didn't do much damage since all I had on my feet were worn-out tennis shoes. I discarded the wood as I walked back to the gas station. Butch was there in the dark. He asked me what happened. "I'll tell you tomorrow."

The pent-up anger I had toward this young man had been building up the entire trip. I never felt bad about what I did to this guy. I think back about the teenager with the black glasses who whispered, "Be careful." He was afraid of him. The pool-room teenagers were probably all snickering amongst themselves after what happened to the bully, Mr. Flattop.

I believe bullying is learned at an early age. Their size and appearance generally seem to be involved in the development of bullies. They pick on smaller or less attractive people. It must make them feel powerful.

My uncle bought me boxing gloves to learn how to fight. My Black friend Dylan said, "Forget about the gloves, you need to learn when to run." He was correct since boxing is a controlled violence. Street fighting has no controls, and he who hits first usually wins.

I remember, getting off the city bus in Compton with my sister, it was a daily challenge coming home from school. I would tighten my shoelaces and roll up my pant legs for the sprint home. The four or five guys were lurking somewhere to empty my pockets.

I said, "Do you see them?"

She said, "No."

"Hold my bag," I said as I jumped out the rear door and headed for the alley, and hopefully would clear the picket fence in my backyard.

No luck. I caught my cuff on the top of the picket and was hanging there when I heard my mom yell, "What are you running from?"

I learned to hit first then run. The four guys behind me were all laughing but they didn't get me.

MAP OF MISSOURI

1965

Another typical flat tire.

DAY 23

SUNDAY, MAY 23

NO MORE POOL HALLS

Iola, Kansas, to Collins, Missouri
100 Miles

I had to quietly leave the gas station during the pitch-black night. I found an abandoned house down the road and slept on the porch. We were treated to a beautiful sunrise and a fresh-air ride through the farmlands of Kansas and Missouri that day. I saw Butch go flying by and almost waved him down. Nah, I'll catch him in a few miles. If he was racing again, he would win when he found out I was behind him. Finally, I caught up with him some miles out. We stopped and decided to finish this trip together since we couldn't do it alone.

During the sixties, there was always confusion when you mentioned having a bike. The bicycle craze had not started yet so when you said, "I have a bike," people assumed you had a Honda, Harley, or some brand of motorcycle. Hence the confusion.

A few miles farther east, we were flying with the wind. A cop car pulled up next to us with two officers inside. They asked if we had seen any guys on motorcycles pass us.

"No," I said, "but early this morning, at sun-up, we saw two guys on motorcycles heading west out of town." I asked what happened. The cop said two guys assaulted one of their teenagers in town last night. They quickly turned their red lights on and did a U-turn.

Butch finally said something nice. "He deserved it, Norm." Luck—sometimes, you just need to be lucky!

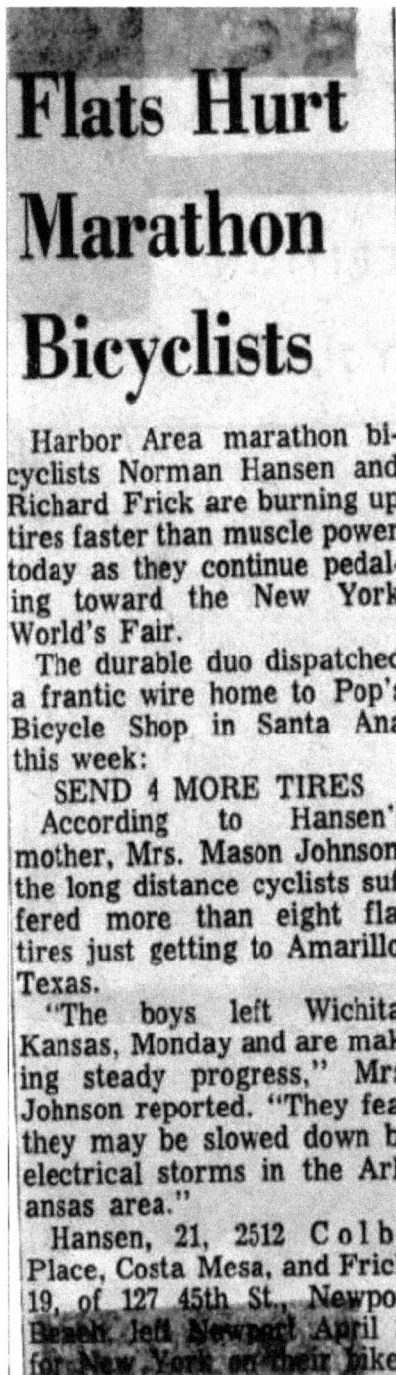

Flats Hurt Marathon Bicyclists

Harbor Area marathon bicyclists Norman Hansen and Richard Frick are burning up tires faster than muscle power today as they continue pedaling toward the New York World's Fair.

The durable duo dispatched a frantic wire home to Pop's Bicycle Shop in Santa Ana this week:

SEND 4 MORE TIRES

According to Hansen's mother, Mrs. Mason Johnson, the long distance cyclists suffered more than eight flat tires just getting to Amarillo, Texas.

"The boys left Wichita Kansas, Monday and are making steady progress," Mrs Johnson reported. "They fear they may be slowed down by electrical storms in the Arkansas area."

Hansen, 21, 2512 Colb Place, Costa Mesa, and Frick 19, of 127 45th St., Newpor Beach, left Newport April 3 for New York on their bikes

DAY 24

THE FARM

Collins, Missouri, to Camdenton, Missouri

55 Miles

We rode past Cottey College in Nevada, Missouri—an art school for girls. We met a young guy on the side of the road who had heard about our trip from the local news. We mentioned we should stay at the girls' school. He laughed and told us they were gone on summer vacation. We were smelly and unshaven and decided not to think about it.

He offered for us to stay at his grandmother's farm. His young mother had just passed away and he was now living with his grandmother in Collins, Missouri—not on the original map. It is east of Nevada, Missouri. The farm was something you would see in a magazine: a big, white two-story house with barns and tractors on two hundred acres. I had never been on a farm and neither had Butch. There was an outside pump for filling a bucket and we actually used a metal dipper to drink the water. I had never drank well water and was amazed at how cold it was.

We sat up half the night in the barn talking about the beaches in California. The guy had never been on a beach. *The Beach Boys* were popular in 1965 and they were from Huntington Beach. He was fascinated with surfing, etc. Anyway, thank you, Dennis Smith from Collins, Missouri.

Hand pumping well water.

DAY 25

RIDING FATIGUE—CB RADIOS

Camdenton, Missouri, to Jefferson City, Missouri
60 Miles

We departed the farm after Dennis's grandmother fixed us a huge breakfast; eggs from the chicken coop, slabs of bacon, whipped butter from a churning device. It came from their cows on the farm. The butter was pale-looking and tasted almost sweet. There was also canned peaches from one of those mason jars. Best breakfast ever.

The ride started with thirty-five to forty mph wind to our right side. The wind and the constant out-of-the-seat, up-and-down dancing on the pedals was just painful. This was going to be a tough ride with those rolling hills. I'm not sure we even were averaging ten mph most of the day.

Road construction had just started for the summer all over the country and we were starting to see detour signs—that was not a good sign!

We went swimming in the Niangua River and had no soap—darn! It's a part of the Ozarks water system.

Riding in these hills made it difficult to find the correct gear to be in. It was difficult to hear the big trucks coming but, we found out later, they always knew where we were. They would blare their horns miles away, so we always had time to get off the bikes and hold on to things so they would not blow away. That was nice of them.

When we stopped at the next truck stop, the truckers told us that they had twenty-two channels on their CB radios and would talk to each other about our positions with mile markers. Those truckers were life-savers. They would always buy us cokes, candy, and tease us about our tight, black riding shorts. "Hey!" they would yell out, "We can see your nuts hanging." We would all laugh.

Can you imagine wearing Walkman radios with plug-in earpieces, listening to music? We would be dead! Nothing but a grease spot on Niangua Route 54.

That night we finally found an empty house and rolled out our dirty bags under a porch. It rained all night and I, with a bit of bad luck, managed to find a place that got wet, but I kept it from Butch. Lightning struck all night. If only we had access to drugs, alcohol, or better yet, pain pills. We usually changed from our riding shorts into our long corduroy pants. We used our jackets on top of our carry-back bags for a pillow. I'm not sure, based on the journal, that I slept more than two hours at a time. I was having problems writing in the journal about the previous day's events. It kind of scared me.

It may have been from severe fatigue, lack of sleep, or improper hydration. Memory loss at this age was scary.

One question frequently asked is, "What motivated you to keep going?" There were times while pedaling and daydreaming that the thought of quitting came into my head. If we quit, we might forever be saddled with not accomplishing what we promised. It could haunt us later in our life. Regrets I didn't need in my future. Finishing last is better than not finishing at all.

DAY 26

WEDNESDAY, MAY 26

"ELECTROLYTES"

78 Miles

These rolling hills were beating us down to utter exhaustion.

We stopped at the Bagnell Dam and I took pictures of this part of the Ozark water system. Back then, we were unaware of electrolyte depletion. Although we were drinking a lot of water, as I can see from my journal entries, the effects of low electrolytes took its toll on our systems—headaches, fatigue, lack of sleep, and impaired judgment. We just weren't educated about any of this. Today, there are products—Gatorade, etc. We just didn't know what our liquid intake should have been for this type of daily, grueling riding. The Tour de France was a big event, but those kinds of cycling events had not started here in the States.

That night, we were invited to stay at the Salvation Army in Jefferson City, Missouri, and we accepted. Their cots, showers, and food were more than welcomed. I weighed myself and I was 153 pounds; I had lost ten pounds. That's a lot when you see our bodies already appeared to have zero body fat.

We met a thirty-one-year-old fellow in Jefferson City who just got out of the service after twelve years as a master sergeant. He was riding to California and had left New York five weeks ago. He was taking his time and staying in motels nightly. He had a backpack on and a one-speed bike with fenders. He would never make it over the Continental Divide with that kind of poor equipment! His whole story made no sense. Anyway, we just said "Good luck." He would need it.

We finally got a night's sleep with real pillows, a situation unlike our usual jacket over our black carry bags—this insured a stiff neck in the morning.

DAY 27

THE PHONE

Union, Missouri to St. Louis, Missouri
55 Miles

We stayed in Union, Missouri, at the city jail and did laundry at four a.m. We wanted to arrive early to be able to take pictures of the Mississippi River Crossing. I finally figured out why we had no pictures in the late afternoon or evening. The camera was a Kodak 127 mm and had no flash attachment. Butch would send the rolls of film for developing to Newport Beach from the post office in towns we would ride through.

Butch was increasingly upset about Stephanie. He was in love with this girl who was our age. Her parents allowed her to live in a guest house which was behind their big house on Lido Isle. We would go over to her house in the late evening. Her parents could not stand either of us. My mother was Evelyn, the barber on 32nd Street. His father was the plumber on 46th Street. Not a good match for the Lido Isle class. Her parents were trying to get her nose fixed. She did not like the shape of it. My thought was the nose job wouldn't help that much.

We would call home when we found an available payphone. It was difficult to find a payphone that worked, and if it did work, you needed to put the correct change in to get a person-to-person call. *If the operator could get your person*

74

on the phone. Butch would call Stephanie but she was never there. Butch was noticeably upset. I would call the barber shop my mother owned to collect and report where we were. The phone service was marginal at best if it had not been broken into to get the money out.

MAP OF ILLINOIS

1965

500 Mile Race — Indianapolis, Ind.
The first lap of the world famous 500 Mile Memorial
Day Race.

Ektachrome by J. Herbert Elliott

Hi - why did'nt
you write me in st Louis?
Henry said he Talked
to you. If something
came up and you are
afraid to tell me please
Tell me in New York
at Post Office. Trying
To make it To RACE?
say hi to DAN & Everyone
Tell Jim Curtiss to have
my money when I get
Back because I'll be Real
Brock!! he could make it to
N.Y. in 5weeks But I'll probably extend it To
6 weeks. see you Norm.

Post Card

Mason +
Evelyn Johnson
2512 Colby Pl.
Costa Mesa
California.

75406-B

DAY 28

GATEWAY TO THE WEST

St. Louis, Missouri, to W. Carlyle, Illinois
60 Miles

Like most big cities, traffic was a problem crossing the bridge. I had no idea it was so wide. The bridge must have been two miles long.

We were scheduled to stay at a Schwinn bike dealership owner's house. I believe his name was Gil Champs. We also picked up supplies at the main post office. I received my new riding shorts, tires, and the photos Butch had sent to Newport to get developed. The pictures came out great and some are in the album. Unfortunately, Butch was disappointed that Stephanie had not sent him a card or letter. Here we come, Mr. Payphone. I was quiet and did not say a word. He was hurting!

We went back to the shop and they were working on our bikes—turning wheels, new brake pads, cleaned chains, and tightened derailer cables. The rear-wheel, five-speed clusters had small ball bearings in them. I was a bit concerned about the lack of maintenance and dirt we had gone through. The guys at the shop said that the year before, at this time, two Japanese guys on similar bikes from Japan had come through. They were heavily laden with clothes and packs on the front as well as the rear. They looked strong and were also on their way to New York. They could have been on publicity thing as well. We went to a large park on Arsenal Street. The guy at the park said a wealthy man donated the land and gifted money for annual maintenance and up-keep. The stipulation was that no Negroes were allowed in the park. Talk about discrimination. (When you are our age, you don't confirm anything. Anyway, it's in the journal so could it be true?) I know the country was talking about integration, but hell, we had no idea what that meant. There were no Black people at Newport Harbor High or Costa Mesa High. The next day, we rode again with no idea of what to expect.

"Arrived in St. Louis yesterday, early A.M. and crossed the mighty Mississippi River. Butch took a unique picture of me on the bridge with the middle of the arch section not finished" (quote from journal).

As you can see from the map at the beginning of the chapter, we decided to ride to Indianapolis for the Indy 500 race. As I mentioned previously, stupid decisions don't take long to make. Another galactically stupid decision.

Along Highway 40, we stopped and were told by the locals that it was almost impossible to get tickets since the tickets were sold the prior year.

Between finding a place to sleep and storing the bikes, we didn't have enough money. It made no sense. We were on schedule to reach New York and this would mean an additional two days so back to Highway 50. Just a mere one-hundred-mile detour on bikes!

MAP OF INDIANA

1965

DAY 29
DETOURS

W. Carlyle, Illinois, to Vincennes, Indiana

108 Miles

We spent most of the day stopping for paving-operation detours. It was getting late, so we started looking for a park. We found a park in West Carlyle, Illinois—not on our original map.

We got chased out by the caretaker: "No camping!" So, we went farther into the park. He must have called the cops because we saw a cop car cruising around. We played hide-and-seek for a while. We won!

One thing about cops in patrols cars at night: they do not want to get out in a pitch-dark park with a flashlight. They are afraid to step in a piece of dog shit and then smell dog shit all night in the patrol car. There was no leash law and, in those days, no poop bags supplied at the parks. My neighbor, who was a cop, told me that the best place to hide from cops was in the park!

We took pictures of the Lincoln historical trip westward at age twenty-one. Butch is sitting on the memorial. You probably could not do that today.

Look at this detour!

DAY 30

DETOURS

Vincennes, Indiana, to Bedford, Indiana

70 Miles

There was beautiful foliage along the highway. Although we were filthy, every river crossing was not inviting enough to swim in; dark, dirty, green moss covered the water's edge.

I guess the farther east we went, the worse the country looked. Growth seemed to have scared nature, although in some places, conservation was implemented to try and preserve whatever nature possible. It's inevitable that unbridled growth in buildings, roads, and bridges will have an impact on our environment. I saw it as I rode along.

Yes, that is me on an oil and tarred road. Great detour! We used gasoline at the next gas station to remove the oil-based tar from our wheels, spokes, tires, and the bottom of our shoes. The upside of this event was that we smelled of gas rather than the usual smell we had become accustomed to.

Anybody who saw this was less likely to complain about roads. What a mess!

Not much room for two guys on bikes and two trucks passing with soft gravel on the shoulder of the narrow road.

MAP OF OHIO

1965

Hamilton

Lake Erie

Windsor

Westfield

Erie

Jamestown

Ashtabula

Toledo

Cleveland

Sandusky

Warren

Youngstown

Bryan

Fremont

OHIO TPK. (TOLL RD.)

Nor-walk

Findlay

Van Wert

Akron

Massillon

New Castle

Lima

Marion

Mansfield

Canton

Steubenville

O   H   I   O

Delaware

Cambridge

Washington

Springfield

Columbus

Wheeling

Piqua

Zanes-ville

Richmond

Dayton

Chillicothe

Marietta

Athens

Bloomington

Cincinnati

Hillsboro

Parkersburg

Covington

Portsmouth

Madison

Gallipolis

Maysville

New Albany

Jeffersonville

Ashland

Huntington

Ohio Riv.

89

ROCKY FORK TRUCK STOP - Rt. 50 & 753, Hillsboro, Ohio

Sinclair gas station and café

DAY 31

The Crank Issue

Bedford, Indiana, to Cincinnati, Ohio
85 Miles on Hwy 50

No more detours this day. We were seeing more traffic and small towns, along the way. Some were not on the map. They weren't really towns—a gas station, a few stores, laundromats. There were a lot of places to stop to eat and drink. I was down to about ninety dollars at this point. Of course, no protein bars! We were moving along at a good pace. Not as many hills but not flat either. We were always tired!

The next morning, we were lying in our bags as usual under a picnic table when I heard Butch say, "What the hell is this?" When he rolled over, he noticed the crank-arm length that was stamped "170 mm Strada" on the bike he was on. Both bikes were set up as duplicates, so we could at least have one bike if the other was broken, and we could switch parts. Only one item was not the same. It was the crank-arm length. The other bike was stamped "165 mm Strada." He accused me of giving him the bike that was harder to pedal so I would be stronger in the long run and have more energy. I was now used to his outbursts and competitive attitude. I quickly said, "After two thousand, five hundred miles, what difference does it make now since we both look like shit and feel like shit. I'll switch bikes if that's what will make you happy." I was met with dead silence and the usual hate glare. Now he was confused about which one to take. Good! You readers can do the math and decide if 5 mm makes any difference in three thousand miles!

The cadence of crank arms going around is easier with a 165 mm Strada crank arm. It's easier when pedaling uphill. The climbs up the Continental Divide and the Appalachian Mountains would be easier, and you would burn fewer calories. His constant bickering about minor issues were always a mental nuisance for me. The pollution of road from passing cars in our face, poor food, poor hydration, and ever-present pain were grating on our attitudes toward each other.

Cincinnati was another big, stinky city. We had smog back then and there was the usual exhaust smell from cars, trucks, and buses. We always tried to avoid staying in the big cities. Too many cars, people, buses, and train tracks, so we would find a place before the city or after to sleep. The highways always went through big cities. There weren't any bypass highways. I would try and find a barber shop to get a shave. Butch was lacking in facial hair. So, we just cruised through the city and found a barbershop.

DAY 32

Cincinnati, Ohio, to Campground
104 Miles on Hwy 50

It happened to be the year of the cicadas. They come out of hibernation approximately every two decades. Like most people, I thought they were grasshoppers, but they're not. They are called "periodical cicada." They swarm between seven and seventeen years. The year 1965 marked the seventeen-year swarm. How lucky were we!

When they hit you, they would make a sound like a scream. They're about the size of a fifty-cent piece. They're black with bright orange stripes. We had to deal with them all the time, and since we had long hair, they were always getting stuck in our hair. There were millions of them, and they drove us nuts for hundreds of miles. Worst of all, they were run over by cars and would get up into our brake pads. What a mess.

At night, there was a constant buzzing from the cicadas along with all other kinds of animal sounds. We got used to it and always fell asleep. We headed into the Appalachian Mountains of West Virginia next. Hopefully, we could get rid of these constant guests in our hair.

We stopped for the night someplace between Hillsboro, Ohio, and Parkersburg, West Virginia, at a campground, and three nice families fed us dinner. We finally got into our bags when we started hearing growling in a large bush some thirty feet away from us, which turned out to be some animal. By this time, we were sleeping on top of the picnic tables to keep rodents out of our bags. The brazen little bastards would crawl through the black carry bags we used for pillows and chew away at our peanut butter sandwiches. They seemed to wait until we were asleep.

The riding was starting to get difficult again with sharp ascending hills as we approached the west side of West Virginia.

Marathon Rider Home

Beatle-like Biker Got 'Bugged'

By TOM FORTUNE
Of the Daily Pilot Staff

Newport Beach marathon bicyclist Richard "Butch" Frick is home from New York City today, looking like a golden-haired Beatle who in fact had tangled with some real live bugs.

Frick, 19, stepped from the Greyhound bus in Newport Wednesday afternoon with flowing hair to be greeted by his mother and dad, Mr. and Mrs. Victor R. Frick, 127 45th St., his sister, Karen, 15 and girlfriend, Terry Pantzar, 17.

The marathon rider and his partner, Norman Hansen, 21, 2512 Colby Place, Costa Mesa, left Newport on bikes April 31 and arrived in New York 42 days later.

Frick let his hair grow into flowing locks because he won't let anybody but Hansen's parents cut it, Mr. and Mrs. Mason Johnson, who operate a Newport barber shop.

But the Beatle-like hair proved a real problem, Frick said, when he and Hansen encountered some real bugs during three nightmarish days in the Ozarks.

It happened to be the year of the locusts, who come out of hibernation every two decades, and the irksome bugs got caught in the youths' hair and beards (Frick arrived home clean shaven).

"They're big black bugs like 50-cent pieces with bright orange stripes, and when they hit your face they scream,"

Frick recounted to the amazement of his sister and girlfriend.

"We were only wearing riding shorts and shoes, and the air was thick with them. Like most people I thought locusts were grasshoppers, but they're beatles."

Frick thought New York was "all right." The cyclists went to the World's Fair, Greenwich Village, the Empire State Building, and rode their bikes across the Brooklyn Bridge. They stayed with Rose Deady in Flushing, a second cousin of Hansen.

Along the road the vagabonds slept outdoors, in jails, and an amusement park, and one night during a hailstorm

in a restroom at a filling station.

Hansen will arrive in Santa Ana this afternoon, as his parents continue their own eastward trek to Arkansas.

Frick will meet him for a publicity call to Pop's Bicycle Shop, 118 S. Main St., which outfitted them with spare tires and wired ahead part replacements.

Not for another three weeks, when Hansen's parents, Mr. and Mrs. Mason Johnson, 2512 Colby Place, Costa Mesa, return, will Frick submit to a haircut.

Frick would have talked on, but his father cut the interview short. "Want to hit the shower now son?" he asked.

For an answer he got a nod from a weary head.

WEST VIRGINIA
1965

Washington

Wheeling

250

88 · Morgan town

165 · Cumberland

Fairmont
Clarksburg

227

Riv.

50

250

219

50

11

Winche

Parkersburg

Ohio

21

Weston

W E S T

220

SHENANDOAH

19

Elkins

V I R G I N I A

246

MTNS.

Huntington

23

Charleston

Gauley Br.

119

128

181

Logan

*WEST
VIRGINIA
TURNPIKE
(TOLL RD.)*

60

19
21

Lewis-
burg

White
Sulphur
Sprs.

52

19

APPALACHIAN

Princeton
Bluefeld

19

Entering scenic West Virginia

DAY 33

Parkersburg, West Virginia, to Clarksburg, West Virginia

80 miles, Hwy 50

After eighty miles of tough hills, we finally made it—Clarksburg, West Virginia. The roads were winding uphill and downhill sweeps with sharp turns. The next few days were going to be tough in these mountains. We had an incident with a driver telling us to get the fuck off the road. We were advised that there were hillbillies in these mountains who ran whiskey. Anyway, they had ponytails and looked like back-home hippies. Our friends the cicadas were still with us.

Clarksburg, West Virginia, was in a dry county. It meant all liquor stores were state-owned and no beer or liquor was sold after twelve p.m. There were after-hour clubs, or bootleg bars as they were called. The cops were paid off along with the district attorney. They also had whorehouses and a bridge called "Prostitutes' Bridge." This was a rough place we were told, by a guy named Ray Love. As it turned out, he would be our guide for a night on the town. I'm not sure I believed too much that came out of his mouth. Neither Butch nor I had ever seen a whorehouse or a prostitute in Newport Beach. We were very naïve!

I noted in my journal, "I think whenever the laws are too strict, the more problems the police and government have in controlling all phases of crime."

We picked up two pretty girls—or rather they picked us up and invited us to their house the next day. Butch was out with one of them at one point, so hopefully this thing with the girl back home was not eating at him anymore.

We never made it to the house the following day, and I managed to get rid of the guy who was promoting women to us. Yes, it was a narrow escape, since they might have tried to rob us.

2 Bicyclists Due at Fair On Weekend

After battling their way through an invasion of locusts clogging West Virginia highways, Harbor Area marathon bicyclists Norman Hansen and Richard "Butch" Frick are expected to reach the New York World's Fair Friday or Saturday, it was reported today.

Last word received here from the cross-country riders indicated they were leaving the Applachian Mountains region.

Hansen, 21, of 2512 Colby Place, Costa Mesa, and Frick, 19, of 127 45th St., Newport Beach, left the Harbor area and headed for New York on April 31.

They have worn out 10 sets of tires on their foreign built racing machines.

MAP OF VIRGINIA

1965

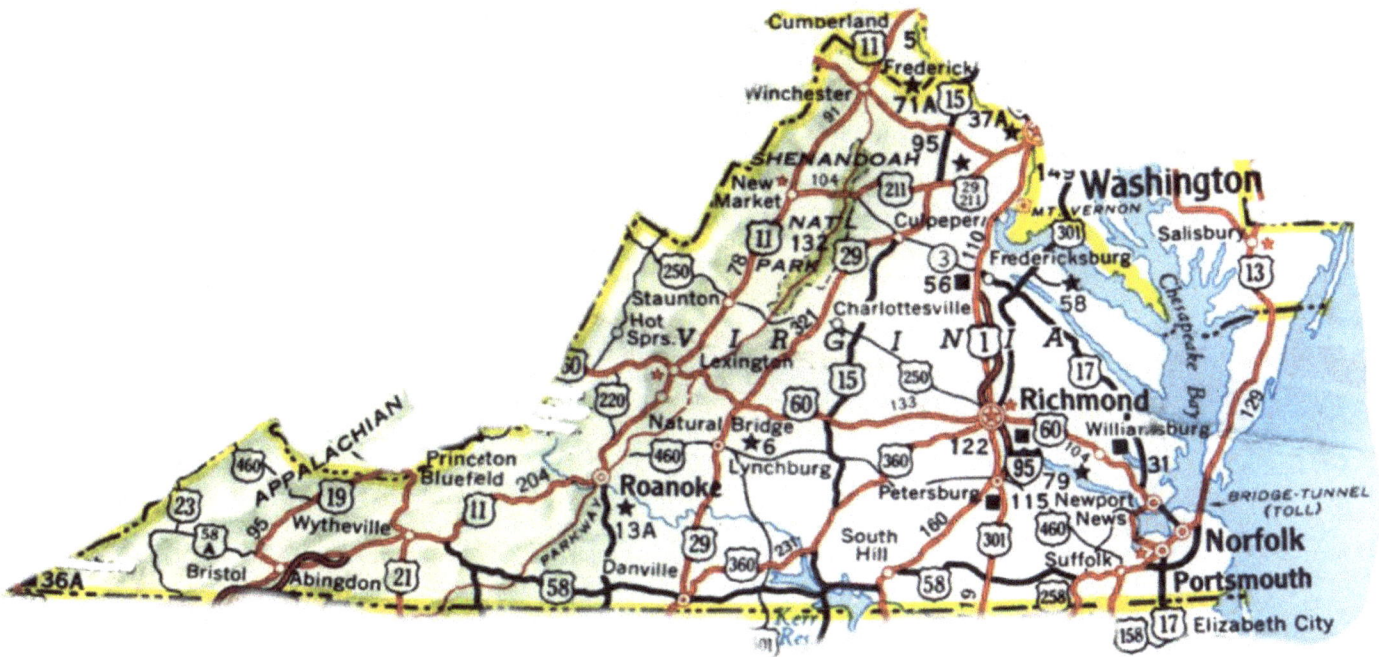

We stopped at a Civil War marker.

DAY 34

Clarksburg, West Virginia, to Winchester, Virginia
170 Miles on Hwy 50

We had a late departure the next morning after news media and TV men took pictures and asked the same old question: "Why are you guys doing this?"

The Appalachian Mountains were very colorful, but the weather was quite peaceful that time of the year. The altitude sign read 2,900 feet. It was still very humid. The cicada were still with us, but not nearly the millions as in previous days.

The marker was for Thornbury Bailey Brown, 1868. He was the first Union soldier to die here, generally considered the first Union soldier to die in combat.

We were sitting in Fellowville Roadside Park. We would be in Winchester by the next day or the following Monday. I called home the previous night and was told I had been accepted to California State, Long Beach, for the fall term. How was I going to pay for the tuition? I was happy about my acceptance to Cal. State, Long Beach. My issues as I rode were concerned with what to study. I had to find a career path that would lead to employment. Waiting tables and mowing lawns did not meet my expectations for income.

Growing up in Newport Beach, where there was no exposure to poverty and you were constantly surrounded with pure wealth, was confusing to a twenty-year-old. The only things I would inherit were a few antiques of my mothers.

This pedaling and constant daydreaming would soon end. Then what was I going to pedal? Yikes!

A lot of people we met there had bad teeth. The locals said it's the hard water they drink. It rained and snowed there, but they said they weren't damming up enough drinking water. Most were on well water.

Still Pedaling

Marathon Riders Nearing New York

Harbor Area marathon bicyclists Norman Hansen and Richard "Butch" Frick were shceduled to leave Philadelphia today on the final lap of their pedal-powered journey from Newport Beach to the New York World's Fair.

The youths, who have been on the road 42 days now, reported to their parents here that they expect to pedal onto the fairgrounds in the Empire state some time tomorrow.

So far in their cross continent bicycle ride, the Harbor area duo has overcome more than a dozen tire failures, brushes with speeding motorists, swarms of locusts and finally, a bout with food poisoning.

They are also running out of money.

Pedaling out of the Appalachian Mountains in West Virginia, the bike riding pair had to slush t.. ir way through an infestation of locusts covering the pavement.

Just outside Philadelphia, Frick suffered an attack of food poisoning and the pair was forced to rent a motel room overnight, thus further deflating their cash reserves. Hansen now has $5 left and Frick, $35.

Frick, 19, of 127 45th St., Newport Beach, and Hansen, 21, of 2512 Colby Place, Costa Mesa, left Newport April 31 on their cross-country bike ride.

DAY 35

FOOD POISONING

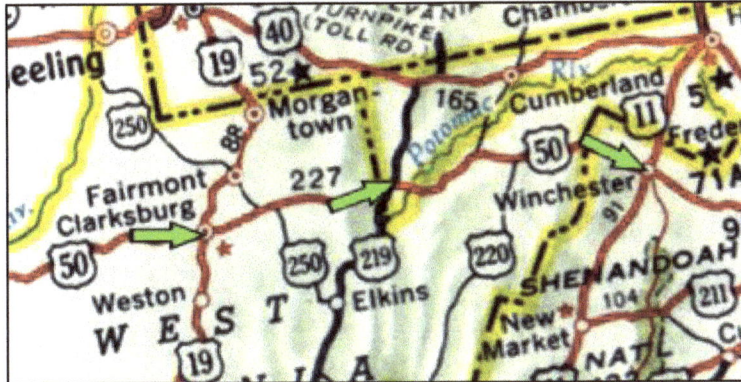

Crossing the Potomac River

It was approximately 170 miles from Clarksburg, West Virginia, to Winchester, Virginia. We had crossed the Potomac River.

I noticed my ass was half on and half off the bike on that bridge. We had to ride on the Bridge's sidewalk, as you can see why from the picture.

We finally got into the river and it was cold, even in June.

Sometime in the late afternoon, Butch got sick—throwing up and heaving his guts out. I was scared because he was pale. It was either from food poisoning, fatigue, or worse yet, the Asian flu! The Asian flu scare pandemic was still in the US in 1965.

We found a motel someplace near Winchester, Virginia, that we could get into for six dollars, with two beds and a shower. Butch ate a little something, showered, and got into bed at eight p.m. Morning would tell his condition. I hoped he made it.

Riding through Virginia on our way to Gettysburg, Pennsylvania.

MAP OF PENNSYLVANIA

1965

Wednesday, June 9, 1965
160th day – 205 days follow

125 Miles

Passing Through Gettysburg. The place we sleeped at was part of The Third picket of The Great Battle. The smell of maple leaves and the falling cotton wood blossoms seem to bring you within The realm of the people The way They were 100 years ago. Hand To Hand battle would seem some To be The most fearful as well as bloodiest. Approx. 40,000 men died at This battle. At That time Not a Tree!! Rode Like Hell To day. Sleeped in Norristown. We Last night out I am disappointed because it ended so quickly. Got the Last bunch of pictures from N.Y. Post office. A freeway no use Than L.A. was where we Traveled and Finally got To the N.J. Turnpike close To holland Tunnel To Find out we were not allowed and would eventually end up Taking a Taxi to ~~~~ st. Island and Then across N.J. Ferry To see Those powerfull buildings close Us off from California. Awesome sight.

Thursday, June 10, 1965
161st day – 204 days follow

Well we made it. So This is the city. I am depressed. Arrived Approx. 7 o'clock, at St. George Hotel. Rode The subways To Flushing Trying To get To Rose Deedy's house The subway is Fast with Thousands of people Riding. This place is Also a zoo like most of the Big cities we have been in. We Really push it Trying To get here. Last night while on subway platform a man was Telling me about seeing a young, drunk russian get his head severed off while Leaning over platform. He said that for Approx. 15 seconds The man still stood There while his head rolled down the platform. At That time he was 10 years old and It seem humorous but as he grew older It became a sore spot in his life. Youth seems To hide alot of the deep pitfals of glowing up. These trains travel 90 miles an hour.

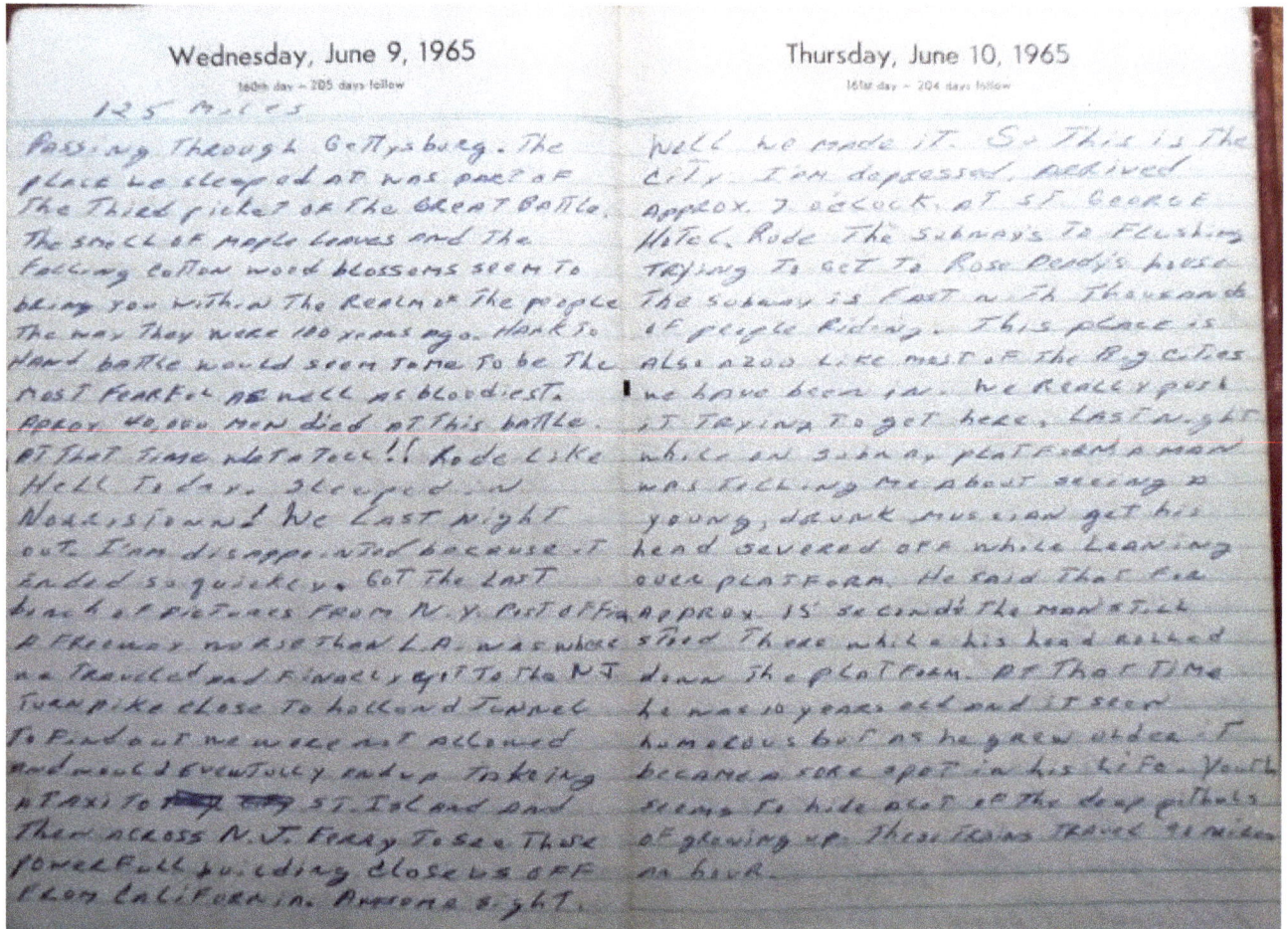

*From overnight stay in Gettysburg Battlefield
from red diary.*

DAY 36

SATURDAY, JUNE 5

MAJOR BIKE FAILURE

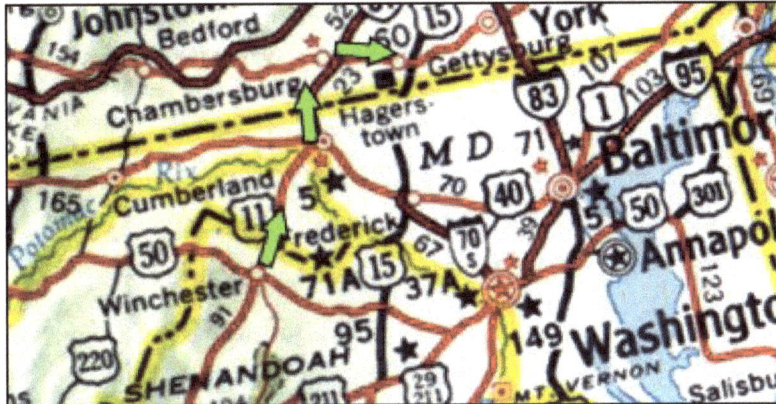

Winchester, Virginia, to Gettysburg, Pennsylvania
105 miles on Hwy. 11

We left the motel late, at eleven a.m. Butch was better but weak. About twenty miles from the motel, the rear Regina five-speed cluster broke on his bike and Butch could not ride. Winchester was the nearest big town with a bike shop. The rear wheel cluster needed a special tool to remove it from the wheel, which we did not have. And, of course, it was raining.

We decided that I would ride to the bike shop in Winchester, Virginia. He would call them from the gas station, where he hoped to get a ride to Winchester. We got to the shop and they couldn't fix it. They sent us to the next bike shop a few miles up on Hwy 11. They had a cluster and replaced it. Just plain lucky!

We slept somewhere outside Winchester, Virginia. We were now in the Shenandoah Mountains and would be riding downhill the next day.

I was exhausted and probably felt worse than Butch, who was quiet and hurting.

107

MAP OF MARYLAND

1965

Norm at Maryland state line.

DAY 37

LAUNDROMATS

Gettysburg, Pennsylvania

At this point, I was too lazy to write. The journal became sketchy.

I had ten dollars left. It was downhill with sharp turns and the pace was fast, thirty-five to forty-five mph, and we were scaring the heck out of drivers.

"Hey, you guys are crazy!" from a passing car. They were correct. I could see the end to this crazy journey with mixed feelings.

Butch was still feeling bad, although he seemed to enjoy riding in the rain as I did.

We made it to the outskirts of Gettysburg. It was about eight p.m. and almost dark. As I recall, we were going to sleep in a baseball dugout, in a local park as usual.

Then, a young pretty girl named Karin stopped and, as others had been, was fascinated with the two of us. We looked terrible, but she took us to her parents' house and put us in the hay loft of their barn. Karin was one of the few nice girls we met. She had just graduated high school and would enter college, unlike the young girl I met in the laundromat in Martinsburg. That girl was seventeen years old with a six-month-old child and married for one year. Her husband had quit high school and was continuously looking for work. She had said, "I'm upset because I've made a mistake and now, I'm sorry." She was a pretty girl with short, jet-black hair and olive complexion. Her eyes were hazel. I think of her often and wonder about the future that was ahead for her.

Throughout our trip, the laundromat was the place we would meet the locals. I would take turns with Butch. He would stay with the bikes and watch the laundry.

I would go off and find a place to eat. This happened all across America. You learn a lot about people, towns, and individual problems. It served us well, and no, we never washed the sleeping bags for fear of ruining them and having to sleep on the bare ground. So, they were discarded when we got to New York. Thank you, Karin Qeisqley, RD3, Gettysburg, Pennsylvania. Her own writing in the journal.

Notice the $100 fine for littering posted on the green sign.

DAY 38

The journal is now void of details. It says we slept on the Gettysburg Battlefield and that I can remember. It was part of the third picket of the great battle. We laid there looking up into the dark sky.

The smell of maple leaves and the falling Cottonwood Blossoms seemed to bring us within the realm of the way people were a hundred years ago as they, too, slept under these same stars preparing for death. Hand-to-hand battle seemed to me to be the most fearful as well as the bloodiest contact. Over fifty thousand men died on that field. What a toll of lost life.

As we lay there, looking up at the dark sky, we tried to see the Early Bird satellite. Just a couple of months earlier, April 6, 1965, the "Early Bird" satellite was launched from Cape Canaveral, Florida. I thought, "What a contrast!"

I guess I, too, died on that battlefield because the entries in the journal are sketchy at best from here on. It was almost over. We are only one hundred miles away. I was tired mentally, physically drained, thin, and dirty. When you are constantly exposed to the elements, your skin picks up road grime, local bugs, dust, and mud, and I guess that's why it's called exposure to the elements. Being constantly dirty was very tough on the brain.

Norristown would be our last overnight before New York.

MAP OF NEW YORK

1965

Butch and Norm on the Staten Island Ferry, going to Manhattan.

DAY 39

THE LAST 100 MILES

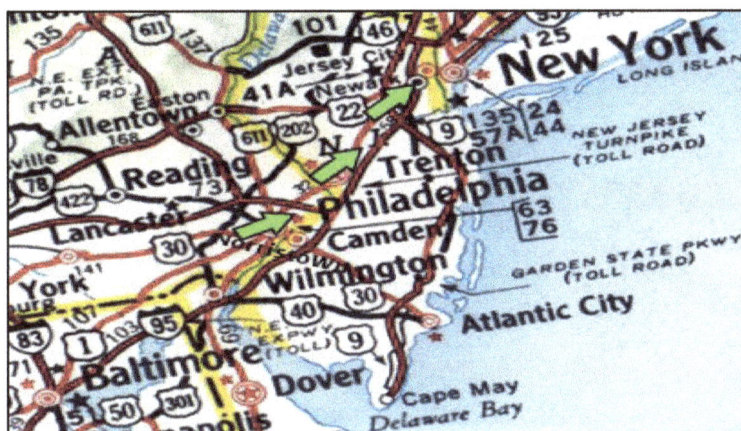

Norristown, Pennsylvania, to New York, New York

"Why is finishing always more difficult than starting?"

Today's ride was fast and furious, slightly downhill, but mostly flat.

We woke early someplace just outside Norristown, Pennsylvania. The roads were dry and the sky was clear of rain clouds. We decided to end this trek today. Unfortunately, the last one hundred miles would turn out to be more difficult than the last three thousand miles.

Welcome to New Jersey! We ended up on some turnpike to find out we could not ride through the Holland Tunnel. Meanwhile, a black limousine with a chauffeur came by and rolled the passenger window down. He told us to get off the turnpike. I told him we were trying to get to Manhattan. His reply was "Take a bus." Well, here came the rage again. The usual "screw you" verbal exchange was made. He stopped the limo and got out with his right hand in his pants pocket. That's it! I was off the bike and reaching for the tire pump. I walked toward him and he looked at my left hand and started backing up. I said, "You want some of my ass?" He quickly jumped back in the limo and took off. Today, I would have been shot. Sometimes aggression works better on aggression. As usual, Butch was leaning against the guardrail, probably hoping I got my ass kicked. Somehow, we ended up on the Staten Island Ferry.

We were really beat up. It was an awesome sight for us to see those huge buildings and realize how little we were.

We got to Manhattan and did not know that the St. George Hotel was in Brooklyn.

No one knew where we were since the 1965 phone system wasn't great and we had not called anyone in a couple of days.

According to the journal, a taxicab driver saw us at the ferry terminal and said, "You guys look like you could use some help."

I said, "We are lost." He took pity on us and drove us to the St. George Hotel. He heard about two guys on bikes and could not believe it was us. Funny thing he said was, "You know the hotel is in Brooklyn, right?" I thought, *Where the hell is Brooklyn?* We had to disassemble the bikes to get them into the trunk. No bike racks.

Well, we made it! It was seven p.m., Tuesday, June 8.

Harbor Pair Sprint In

Marathon Cyclists Reach New York

Dirty, road weary and nearly broke, marathon bicyclists Norman Hansen and Richard "Butch" Frick pedaled into New York City late Thursday, just 42 days after leaving Newport Beach.

The durable duo from the Harbor Area practically sprinted on their bikes the final leg of their cross-continental ride from Philadelphia to the New York World's Fair.

Then it took them nearly five hours just to get across the city to some clean clothes and a shower awaiting them

at the St. George Hotel.

Even though the young men had survived traffic all across the United States, New York's Finest apparently feared for their lives on clogged New York Streets.

Traffic officers ruled Hansen and Frick off the road. They had to complete their cross-town jaunt in a taxicab.

Hansen and Frick called their parents from Flushing, N.Y. to inform them they'd made it at 9 p.m. (PDT).

Frick, 19, is the son of Mr. and Mrs. Victor R. Frick, 127 45th St., Newport Beach. Hansen, 21, is the son of Mr. and

Mrs. Mason Johnson, 2512 Colby Place, Costa Mesa.

"The boys reported they're tired but feeling fine after getting into some clean clothes," Mrs. Johnson reported.

Frick suffered food poisoning in Philadelphia, causing a one day delay in the long-distance bike ride. So he pressed for a sprint on the last leg to make up for lost time.

The bicycling pair are now resting up with family friends in Flushing. They'll start a round of sightseeing in a day

or two.

Hansen and Frick left Newport headed for the New York fair on April 31. Along the way, they encountered lightning storms, brushes with motorists, and swarms of locusts on the highways in the Appalachian Mountains.

They wore out more than a dozen tires on their foreign-built racing bikes.

Hansen had previous experience in long-distance bicycling. He pedaled from Newport to the Seattle World's Fair. The New York jaunt was Frick's first long distance bike ride.

DAY 42

MY FATHER

I did not want Butch to know what I was doing since he was an adopted child and I was personally ashamed that my father never reached out to me.

I told Butch he was on his own for the day and we would go to the fair the following day.

Sometime that day, I met with Brian Butler, my nephew, and Howard Butler, my mother's oldest brother. My uncle was informed by my mother that I was doing this trip in the hope that my father, after seeing the news articles and publicity, would surface in New York.

Before we left the St. George Hotel, my uncle said, "Are you sure you want to see this?" I had no idea what I was about to see. We took the subway system down to lower Manhattan, called the boroughs or Bowery district, where all the homeless shelters were located.

As we walked along the sidewalk, I saw human beings lying next to others with their urine running out into the street. I had never seen anything like that before.

We came to a shelter and my uncle looked at the book with men's names written in it so they could be identified in the shelter.

There was a chain link fence across the entrance which had a gate and lock.

I was told once you went in, you were not to leave until the next morning. My uncle said, "Look, he was here last night, and we had just missed him."

The gate door was open, and I could see long rows of single beds but no men were in the beds. The smell of urine was awful, and the sheets appeared to have yellow stains. We left.

It would be fifty years later when I found him. As the saying goes, "Be careful what you wish for."

My friend and former classmate Bonnie Langseth, while helping me with this project, said, "Let me try something." She contacted the Manhattan homicide division and sure enough, there it was. He had been murdered in the alley on August 8, 1967. He was stabbed to death and left for dead while sleeping under a truck. The guy driving the truck then ran over him and was arrested for vehicular homicide. The grand jury, however, dismissed the case since he was already dead.

And since his body was never claimed, he was buried in Potter's field in Hart Island, New York, as most unknown or indigents were buried there. Forty-five years old and not far from the shelter, his spirit had left him. I am now free of my burden. I think my mother knew but chose not to tell me for fear it might break my spirit. Parenting is so important and sometimes things are best left unsaid.

FINAL JOURNAL ENTRY

JUNE

THE BIKING IS OVER

I sat there wondering what to do. We were out of money and Butch and I were peering out of a twenty-story window while listening to the constant annoying car horns. I think there is a fine to honk your horn in Manhattan now.

We were watching a big fire near a bridge across from the Statue of Liberty. It was the same pea-soup smog we have in Los Angeles. We got to the fair and met our so-called sponsor.

"And that's the way it is."

—*Walter Cronkite*

DAY 43

THE WORLD'S FAIR

Brian, my nephew on my mother's side, picked us up at the hotel the next morning and we were off to the fair.

Our parents had sent us extra money, so we were flush with greenbacks.

I had noticed my nephew was a little quiet and had few details about our bike-trip sponsor. Butch and I were looking at each other and wondering what was up. We received our tickets for the fair. It was a huge event at a place called Flushing Meadows. We saw a huge building that said Africa on the front. Brian said this was it. It was the African Pavilion Exhibit.

Out walked this white guy dressed in a full safari outfit, complete with pith helmet. He looked like those actors you saw in 1920s movies about the "Dark Continent." Knee high socks, boots, cargo shorts, and a cargo shirt.

He took us backstage and we saw these tall Black guys with spears, dressed in loincloths around their waists. They were waiting to do the Watusi dance or something!

Our sponsor looked at us and I'll never forget what he said: "I wondered why it was taking so long. I thought you guys were riding motorcycles." Butch looked at me and, on the q.t., said, "It's time to go home." We were disappointed with this idiot and not sure if he was joking. He may not have been joking but everybody was confused about bikes.

So, a few days later, we boarded a Greyhound Express bus to California. We managed to blow the money that our parents sent us on drinking and women. We barely had enough for the bus fare. We were back on peanut butter and jelly sandwiches in a smoked filled bus. Yes, that is correct, there were not any non-smoking sections back in 1965, no thanks to the N.O.W. Movement. The National Organization of Women had just informed American Women they were now "self-actualized," so women were taking up smoking on a grand scale. The whole country was now on a smoking binge. The women even had their own brands: Virginia Slims, Vogue, etc.

They were asking men to dance, asking us out, and on some occasions, would ask us to do the horizontal twist (No wonder I was lost and confused). The women's liberation really affected us, and it was not a lack of oxygen! So, I sneezed and wheezed all the way home while listening to Dionne Warwick on a wind-up portable record player that Butch bought at a pawn shop.

Stephanie would not be waiting for him, but the draft board was waiting for me.

Across the country, the question had been: "Why are you doing this?" Then, as it is now some fifty plus years later, it is the same answer: "I was trying to find my father!"

Another question after the trip had finished was, "Did you learn anything from this trip?" Now as I look back, the answer is yes. I learned how big and beautiful our country really is, as I have seen it wheel for wheel. For Democrats, Republicans, Independents, and all individuals, I say take care of our environment before Mother Nature takes care of us.

Harbor Cyclists Head Home

Durable Duo Dump Two-wheelers, Try the Bus

By BILL ROWEN
Of the Daily Pilot Staff

This time leaving the pedaling to someone else, Harbor Area marathon bicyclists Norman Hansen and R i c h a r d "Butch" Frick are returning home Wednesday after their cross-country journey f r o m Newport Beach to New York City.

They are coming home on a bus.

Hansen sold his bike in New York and Frick shipped his home.

"We sent them enough money to buy airplane tickets," reports Frick's mother, Mrs. Victor Frick, "but they said that this time they just wanted to take the bus."

Hansen, 21, of Newport Beach, and Frick, 19, of Costa Mesa, arrived in New York June 11 after spending 42 days on the road from Newport Beach.

New York did not exactly respond with a ticker tape parade. The youths had hoped to appear on TV programs to recoup some of their expenses, but they could not contact any networks or producers.

"They were rather put out that they couldn't call in," Mrs. Frick explained. "All the TV stations said they would have to write a letter before they could be considered for any appearances."

Staying with relatives of Frick in Flushing, the youths gave up show business plans and decided to return home as soon as possible.

Their parents, who had wired them money as soon as they arrived, were surprised by their decision to take the bus, however.

The youths left New York Sunday night, a little over a week after they arrived.

At this moment, Mr. and Mrs. Mason Johnson, Hansen's parents, are on their way to a vacation in Arkansas. According to their calculations, they will cross the youths' path in Albuquerque, N.M., and plans have been made for a brief meeting there late this afternoon.

FREQUENTLY ASKED QUESTIONS

1 **Started on May 1, 1965 and finished on June 11, 1965.**

   a.   42 days with numerous detours.

2 **How many miles per day average?**

   a.   Averaged 80 to 90 miles per day.

3 **Average mileage per hour?**

   a.   12 to 15 miles per hour.

4 **Where did you sleep?**

   a.   Mostly on the ground in sleeping bags. No down bags or down jackets. Bike shoes and tennis shoes.

5 **What type of Bikes?**

   a.   One Schwinn Paramount with 10 speeds and one Bianchi with 10 speeds.

6 **How much gear did you take?**

   a.   Wheels restricted to weight spokes, chain links, tubes, tires, and tools.

   b.   No tent as this was too much weight.

   c.   "See Bike Pictures"

7 **What about food?**

   a.   Peanut butter and jelly sandwiches wrapped in cellophane.

Note: First thousand miles tough as there were no Power Bars or Gatorade.

WHAT WERE THE BIGGEST PROBLEMS FACED?

1   Summer road construction and detours.

2   Dogs – No leash laws back then.

3   Flat tires from glass on the road as there was no "Litter Bug" program started yet.

4   Lack of water.

5   Sun – No SPF 50 sunblock.

6   Sunglasses – No biking glasses then.

7   Remember: No Interstate Highway system yet. See: "Original Map" – All two lane roads with "No" Bike Lanes.

8   No cell phones – public phones only – collect calls to home or Western Union for equipment support.

9   Finding a place to sleep before nightfall. The flashlight died the first night.

10   Sleep deprived, fatigue.

THIS WAS NO VACATION!!!!!!

ACKNOWLEDGMENTS

Parker Hansen (son)

Mark Terry, ESQ—Patent Attorney, Florida

Bruce Schwab—Schwab Cycles, Colorado

Shane Coursen—Let's Talk Graphics, Nevada—Custom Map

Jared Fisher—Las Vegas Cyclery, Nevada

Joe Guercio—Not Your Average Joe, California—Web Design

Bonnie J. Langseth—IT Work, Story & Pictures, Nevada

Dave Parmelee—Photographer, Florida

Emma Pulver—Kelly Printing, Florida

Zuri Zepeda—Kelly Printing, Florida

Ariel Thieken—Cover Designer, Kelly Printing, Florida

David Witt—Restored Photos, Creative Photo of Florida

TJ Homerding—Valley Blueprint, Nevada

THE AUTHOR

Norm Hansen, age 77 in 2020

MAJOR RIDES

1 Newport Beach, California, to Seattle, Washington, 1963 Wrong way, South to North.

2 Newport Beach, California, to New York, New York, 1965 World's Fair.

3 England to Europe, Seven Weeks, 1981.

Two of these trips were done on his 1963 Paramount.